60 Miles from Neiman's

Finding Your Way Back from Others' Expectations

Elian Haan

Elian Haan

ISBN: 979-8-218-04976-8 (Paperback)

ISBN: 978-1-7923-9810-0 (eBook)

Editing by Joppa Editing
Interior design by Ink Drinker Editing and Literary Services
Cover design by Joe Montgomery

First printing edition 2022.

Elian Haan

www.elianhaan.com

"LIFE DOES NOT GET ANY EASIER

YOU JUST GET BETTER AT IT"

Elian Haan

CONTENTS

INTRODUCTION

Hello Friend,

I am so thankful that this book has found its way to you today. My attitude is gratitude. As I was writing this book, my hope was it would find its way to you and anyone who enjoys a story with amusing twists, a dose of situational irony and desired happy endings.

Not only grateful for you, but also for my son. You see, I wanted to share my life story with him, and with little time to give, when would we ever find the time to sit and sift through all these stories?

As an international speaker, life and wellness coach, TV show host, and fitness and yoga instructor, I gave birth to this book to serve Women 40+ who like to get their "sexy" back…and with that I mean feeling healthier, joyful, and staying in a place of overall wellbeing and peace, physically, mentally and emotionally. Sometimes we need to move through trauma and pain that has been stored within for too long. We need to move forwards and move up. I wrote this book to help you with that. Even if you don't know your purpose, this book will connect you with your spiritual self in a new, holistic way, and without buying a plane ticket to India.

It took me a while to dig up the past and all its happenings. As a poor historian who had suppressed enough events, and doing well doing so, I had to recall life changing moments that were deeply hidden because of shame, confusion or even despair. Mostly because I just choose to let go, close my eyes, and choose not to revisit the past. But I am glad I did, as my son, friends and work inspired me to confront my own journeys and start writing my own future adventures. I did exactly that, which led me to believe that we can be the lead player on our own stage. And I love to share that faith I found, in God and myself. I "move" forwards and upwards and want you to do the same.

To make sure you get the most bang for your buck and don't waste any time let's get one thing clear upfront: this book might *NOT be* for you if you believe that:

- You are too old to take on a challenge towards a new habit or spiritual practice.

- It's not sound Christian theology to embrace the mind, body, and spirit connection, and Jesus cares more about your heart than your body.

- God is not a modern thinker and does not own a cell phone

- Being a Jesus-pleaser is the same as being a people-pleaser.

What do you say? Are you still reading? If so, then I cannot wait to go on this journey with you and help you to:

- Reclaim and honor the mental, physical, and spiritual connection as a Christian and "Happy Human" being

- Remember that your body is your best friend, don't abuse it

- Officially drop out of the game of keeping up appearances

- Stop taking things personally

- Remove trauma and pain that has been stored in the body for a long time

- Create healthy boundaries within toxic relationships

- Increase self-trust, self-esteem, and self-love, all while laughing as you learn.

Know that I am here for you as you enjoy reading this story. Please reach out to me for advice, feedback, appointments, and bookings at www.ElianHaan.com , where you find all the links to my Social Media sites as well.

Now, let's turn this page and get to living a life that is strong, fearless, sexy, exciting, and peaceful. Courage, commitment, and success included. Smile

You are a warrior *not* a worrier,

Elian Haan

FOREWORD

A DUTCH TULIP IN DEEP EAST TEXAS

The Dutch seem to have a zest for life and all that it encompasses, at least from my exposure and perspective. Where does an early 60s Vermonter find a lovely young Dutch thing in her late 40s? At the library in Seven Points, Texas. Where else would one look?

The small village of Boekelo (say Boo ka low), Netherlands, rests about two hours east of Amsterdam, very near the German border. It is probably the neatest, cleanest village I have ever seen. Residents sweep their walkways and sidewalks. flowering plants are in window boxes everywhere. There is not a piece of litter in sight. There is an antique train museum, a few small shops, a Texas Steakhouse, and the finest omelet I have ever had in the local café. From here, Elian began her journey through life.

Her parents named her Diane Elizabeth Christina Haan at birth. As is Dutch tradition she was given the nickname Elian, and I have never heard anyone call her anything but Elian. Why not just name her Elian? Don't know. That is just what they do. Elian speaks Dutch, German, English, and French fluently. Since I consider myself a linguist having had three years of French and three years of Latin in high school, plus becoming conversant in Vietnamese courtesy of the U.S. Army, I thought I should learn Dutch. Starting with the alphabet seemed prudent. I quit at the letter g, and have not proceeded further. I can't make those sounds. The Dutch language sounds much like German with guttural utterances but without the arrogance of the Germans.

As with anyone learning a new language, a few idiosyncrasies exist. There is no "th" sound in the Dutch language, and as I could not learn some Dutch sounds, Elian does not pronounce words with this sound as we would. "This and that" becomes "dis and dat." "Other side" (as in a command for Yoga) becomes "udder side," usually much to the delight of participants. Adjectives and adverbs are sometimes used by her in a manner different from Americans: "I have only one hour remaining" becomes "I have one hour remaining only." That is OK, we understand each other perfectly.

She has told me repeatedly the Dutch are the tallest people in the world. Since my college alma mater basketball team has had two seven-foot Dutch centers, I cannot argue with that. The Dutch love herring and consume it with enthusiasm. They put mayonnaise on French fries, and cheese and wine are staples. Cheese shops in Amsterdam are spectacular. Since refrigerators in tiny Amsterdam apartments are very small, they tend to eat out or take out with remarkable frequency. Elian is quite proficient at dining out. She says she can cook but doesn't.

Very early in our relationship I was instructed to read two books: *The UnDutchables* and *The Dutch I Presume?*. My greatest takeaway from this reading is that the Dutch are hoarders. Their attics are full. Elian has so many photos, documents, and mementos of people and times past and present that if she donated them to the Library of Congress, they would have to add a wing. She vehemently denies hoarding and contends they are essential possessions.

Probably the most loving and caring person I have ever known, she cherishes relationships past and present. Her journey through life as an actress, dancer, drug and alcohol rehab counselor, fitness professional, and mother has uniquely qualified her for her life coaching profession. Read on and enjoy her story.

Oh, by the way, it is not pronounced Amsterdam, it is "Awmsterdawm." Learn to pronounce the Dutch alphabet if you can.

By James Taylor, AKA *Mr. Fabulous*

1

THERE ARE NO HASHTAGS FOR THESE MOMENTS

I found myself in the middle of an exciting but emotional weekend, dropping my son off at Norwich University in the state of Vermont. (I live in Texas.) After countless nerve-wracking nights and weeks of shopping and packing only clothes and goods that are on a *four-page* cadet packing list, I found myself exhausted. Seriously, a military university? The last thing I could have ever imagined was my only child moving about 27 hours away, to the other side of the country, let alone a military education, although I was part of the final decision to choose that route and maybe receive an Airforce ROTC scholarship. Norwich University, the oldest private military university and quite a prestigious choice, has one of the most beautiful campuses I have seen, surrounded by the color brush painted mountains of Vermont. My son knew what he wanted and had decided. We went through organizing, preparing, discussions & conversations, giving up hair products, colorfully undies, t-shirt collections, 30-minute showers, and never-ending days with an amazing pack of bright best high school friends...it was finally here. We were in a beautiful Airbnb staring at the hills.

That afternoon a welcome reception, the next morning the "drop off," and a few minutes to hug and love each other. I gave him roots and wings and prepared my son and myself thoroughly. Since he was very young, we said our daily mantra on our way to school in the morning.

"Today is the day; make it a great day."

Famous words from Mel Fisher and myself. I wanted him to believe he could make it, every day. Practicing positive thinking and starting the day with a smile.

That's what I do as life coach and counselor, or working with my patients in addiction recovery, constantly analyzing the situation and trying to avoid a crisis of anxiety, hysteria, or breakdowns. All my life events led up to this, trying to teach and coach and tell others. Bossy type. Is it the wisdom I gathered, willingly or not? The constant desire to share? Wanting to change the world? Maybe it just comes with old age, and it has nothing to do with the results of my struggles and experiences.

Anyway, I taught him, counseled him, explained life, did the 'therapy' thing, all that good stuff. Enough said. Now I leave chances, challenges, curves, choices, adventures, and decisions up to this young man. Yes, he can do it, but what about me? I have encouraged him so much, now it is my time. Just going to enjoy the 'senior' years, lots to do. I am 60 years old and an older mom. Had my son when I was a few days shy of 41 years old. And now almost feeling a bit guilty to be excited about having my time back. Me time, more relaxed, less worried, more time for self, less worried. Is it bad that I feel liberated and free? How do you do it as a mother of three? Or more? I could barely handle the decisions, emotions, and overwhelming loving feeling that comes with having one child...

The last couple of months I had been surrounded by crying and upset moms, at graduation celebrations, at the local stores, at the sports events. Not able to imagine their babies being gone, not able to let go yet. And here I am, so happy, grateful, proud, and excited for him and myself. Full of raw emotions, thinking to myself that I am an egotistical selfish piece of work and most likely abnormal. Not being upset and such. Bad momma. Where are my feelings? Why am I not hysterical? I used to be pretty good at that!

So here I am, excited to be able to start on this book. This book that I promised my son, and he does encourage me constantly. I told him I would tell him about my life. But where do you start? I always think about this little quote my dear friend gave me that sits on the shelf in my bathroom that I love so much. "If you don't do anything crazy when you are young, then you don't have anything to laugh about when you are old." Well, I have more than enough crazy. My life was and is crazy. I am full of life, less crazy, more controlled crazy if there is something like that. Consciously different. Purposely wild. Is it actually ok to be called a rebel when you are sixty years old?

Kids are busy creating in their own little world and then as teenagers, on their way to creating their big, adult world. Kids are not interested in their parents' past lives. Meaning, I don't remember ever asking my mom how or what she went through in her teenage and adolescent years—how she lived, worked, survived and how many stupid things she had done before she saw the light and grew up. Unfortunately, my mom couldn't answer those questions by the time they came to me, that time when I really needed answers and needed her. She passed when I was in my late twenties. When Mama died, I was still relatively naive, impulsive, in an already long lasting, out-of-high-school relationship, studying, working, and way too busy to care. I was tired of my alcoholic parents; meanwhile, of course, thinking that I knew it all.

My son and I did always find quality time to talk, and I would try to prepare him for the next big thing or chapter in his school, sports, and friends' engagements. But did I bring up all this stuff that had happened on my journey? Would I tell him anyway? Do I keep *my past* in the past? The more I gave it a thought, the more it became meaningful to me. My job required for so many years to share my own story, my own experience, the knowledge that came with it. Not fair if more strangers know your past, but not the ones close to you. So yes, I will write for him, and I will tell my story. It will take courage, and I shall not linger. Over the years, many people told me I should write a book, especially if I spoked of my past, or as we shared life lessons. So, this time it is for my son. The one I love, with all my heart, my soul. I did my job raising him; he is flying solo now. One more thing to do. A story to tell. And he is holding me accountable.

2

TO BE VULNERABLE WAS NEVER AN OPTION

"Be strong, I am going to die soon," Mama said. "My alcoholism will kill me if I don't kill myself. You cannot break. You must be the strong one."

I was fourteen. I remember that trip in the car like it was yesterday. We had been in the city, I forget why. We hardly ever went to the city. Mama hated shopping sprees and school supply weekends. We probably had to visit a relative. Out of nowhere came this statement. Well, not surprising from her point of view, as she had now been drinking for a few years, well on her way to become a serious alcoholic, but I was surprised she would share her future plan with me. I remember I answered calmly and very respectfully as I knew she was serious, telling her that I understand she is having a hard time. She knew she would die young and was adamant and willing to prepare me for that event, wanting me to be an adult from that moment on because I was already "wise for my age."

Little did I know I had another fifteen years with my mom, but since that moment I knew she had given up. Tired from fighting her alcoholism, her guilt, her emotions, her pain, her sorrow, and her surroundings. The loss of her brother, her mother—both deaths close to each other in time. The illness or sickness of friends, the unhappiness of others. My mom gave her heart and soul to everyone but also belonged to everyone, as she always made time for others. Our house was filled with people day and night—family, friends, and neighbors. Whoever needed something, Mama would bring it by. Whoever needed a drink, Mama would be glad to join in. The sherry bottles were always filled. And my "aunties," my mom's friends, started their daily visits earlier and earlier.

Now these were the days that a small county town had become a suburban little town. The ladies stayed home and took care of the kids, while dads went to work. It was the early '60s, and it was some sort of a status thing that Mama's didn't have to work. Looking back now, I realize my mom was bored out of her mind and tired of listening to her equally drunk-on-sherry girlfriends. These ladies had probably unhappy marriages, annoying kids, and husbands they couldn't find, literally. What else was there to talk about? Cooking, sharing recipes, and gardening gossip only goes so far. There must have been a reason to gather early mornings around those bottles and fresh baked apple pies before cars and cell phones. For example, my dad would leave the house at 7:30 a.m. and be back at 5 p.m. on the dot. If he was not home at five, Mama would dial the rotary phone, call a local establishment, a bar located on the road between the factory and our house, and confirm with the bartender that he was there. We owned one car, and if Mama needed it, she would bring Dad to work and use the car for her grocery trips or visits with friends. I didn't know why she started drinking more and more. In the beginning, it must have been a social thing. As time progressed, and after her declaration of her upcoming inevitable death (she didn't tell me anything anymore) I started to tell her what to do, or rather, what not to do.

Parents don't discuss their struggles with their little ones, at least not when I was growing up. And although my mom was overly warm and emotional, loving and squeezing everyone with her hugs, she failed to explain to me why, nor did she have to, that she was increasingly dissatisfied with her "perfect" wisteria lane settlement in the newly built suburbs for the expected to be always perfect families. As the dads worked, most young mothers in the neighborhood stayed home to boil tea for the kids after school and make sandwiches. It was the social thing, accepted, in a medium income neighborhood, to be up-and-coming if dads made money and moms stayed home.

I grew up in the most beautiful place. In my memories, our small town was heaven on earth. Endless green pastures with tiny rivers of frog-egg filed waters flowed like strings of beauty among them. Trees would create bows over lanes, and corn fields provided us with snacks and playgrounds. The historic uniquely-shaped milk farms—built with low red or dark V shape roofs and large open rooms in the Middle Ages, where animals and people would live together—were surrounded by green grassland and embraced our small red roof town on all corners and curves. They had closet beds, as my girlfriend from elementary would show me when we would play at her farm. I loved to run in the pastures at her house and chase the chickens. There was so much beauty that you almost take for granted if you moved away and didn't go back to visit frequently. In recent years, I would drive through to dive in the past with my own family, to show them where I had played, walked, and rode my bicycle all over town. My loved ones, being tourists, assured me its beauty is amazing. So clean, so green, and so idyllic. The absolute perfect place to grow up as a child.

We moved to this town and new neighborhood when I was five and my sister was still a baby. We owned the corner house, so our front and side lawn were beautiful and huge, at least in our eyes. Dad had added on to the house so that we had an extra living room, a sunken-in lower part, totally up to date with the "must have" designs of the time. A shaded glass gazebo was added to the back porch, with gorgeous blue morning amethyst blooming and hanging off the sides of it after a few years of growth. I do remember how Mama loved her pots and plants, indoors and out. We even had a cool looking huge built-in masonry brick planter in the middle of the living room, with massive elephant ears, succulents, bromelias, and marble pothos growing everywhere. Mama kept busy with photography, painting, sewing clothes for my sister and me, making carnival and ballet costumes, and, of course, she had her plants. Her artwork and drawings colored my memories. I adored them, adored her. She was the ultimate example of a warm, fun, loving, giving, creative and spiritual being to me. Later, I understood, reading her diaries, that she felt a suffocating loneliness, seemingly socially fine with the ladies, enjoying the more and more earlier alcoholic beverages, but alone in her desire to create and grow spiritually.

Dad was, in my eyes, the hardest working man on earth and had a long-respected job as an engineer with HSA, in our house called Signaal, where they designed naval defense systems, radars, and navigation systems. As an employee for that company, we, as a family, were not able to travel past the German wall. As children, we believed it was because Dad was a spy, super cool and secretive. Dad would blow it off as "it is what it is." Who would be interested in traveling east anyway? No one in their right mind would, according to my parents. They did choose fantastic family vacations. Every year we would find ourselves for a few weeks in Mama's beloved Spain, swimming pools and beaches available at our doorsteps. Dad loved to explore the islands and would rent a scooter with me in the seat behind him, embracing his back. I loved every minute of our summer vacations. It was such quality time with Dad.

Life was perfect for a while, surrounded by loving family members and loved ones. The extended vacations, trips to friends and family, and spending Sundays at my grandma's house. Christmas was filled with real candle lights in the beautiful tree we would get to pick out at the nursery in town. Santa came knocking on the door at the same time my uncle had to run to the store. My maternal grandparents were loving, with a touch of hidden class and royalty in my eyes. My earliest memories of Oma were in her living room playing school with dolls, using match boxes as classroom tables, while she gave me gentle stories and instructions. The first few years of my life Mama and I lived with them, until my parents married. I never saw Oma *not* dressed to the max, always perfectly matching from top to toe, sitting up so straight and walking with perfect posture. Yet, I hardly saw her move about either, as she suffered for as long as I can remember from severe asthma and couldn't wear herself out. Oma taught us table manners, and having to put out the dishes and silverware, I knew how to use a knife and fork at the dinner table.

Opa was the worker, the grocery shopper, the organizer, the caretaker. As much as I looked up to both, I would adore my grandfather for his love and great ideas to entertain us. Sundays in the park are sweet memories, as we would meet up with his two unmarried sisters, Bets and Christien, and feed the ducks all together. These two aunties were very special to the whole family. They lived together in a modest apartment and spoiled all grandkids rotten when they visited the aunties' place. If you are not married after you are 30 years old, you can forget it, I was told. Then you are just destined to stay solo and settle in being a spinster. Unfortunately, I don't remember if they had a life without each other; the two were attached at the hip, and I never saw them alone.

My dad's mother was sturdy, as we would say. Oma Haan was all tough love. A strong, but at times bitter woman, she had lost her husband during an air attack in the war. Even in the '60s, there was still a heavy stamp of World War II on daily life. It was not much discussed, but pain was in the country. You could feel and hear that aftermath lingering. Oma Haan had lost her husband, their car business and car shop, and their attached house by heavy airstrike. The "bomb," as it was referred to, had left her with two little boys, my uncle, and my dad, and she started from scratch after that. Little could we ever imagine what they had been through, like my dad as a young boy, losing his own dad and all he ever knew. However, no one talked about it. Ironic as it sounds at the time, after my sister had been digging in old pictures and articles, we found out that it was not a German bomb. It was the Americans that had accidentally bombed my grandparents' business. All my sister and I knew growing up is that Dad and my uncle were able to go to college, then studied and worked hard to turn their lives around. My uncle ended up in the oil business, and Dad was successful with a great job as an engineer, a cute house in a suburban neighborhood, and a beautiful wife who gave him two beautiful daughters. You would think it couldn't be better.

Mama and Oma Haan did not always see eye-to-eye. As part of the marriage package, I must have contributed to that dismay, but as a child, I did not notice and did not know the truth. After entering her house, my cousins and I grabbed a bar of chocolate from a bottom drawer in the kitchen, played outside, and then went upstairs to investigate the extra bedroom that she rented out to students or young men in need of housing. Since the renters were gone on the weekends, my sister, my cousins, and I would snoop around and smell the ghost of the person in my grandma's house. We always had a great time with my oldest cousin being my age and my youngest my sister's age, so we were definitely a pack. After outdoor adventures we would hit the magazines about the Royal Family, a subscription kept just for us.

As teenagers, on our regular Sunday afternoons at Oma Haan's, we became more aware of her loving but grumpy demeanor. Our favorite television shows, with hip music bands and fast changing colors and lights, would drive her crazy. The editing style and loud music was sinful, too fast for her. According to Oma, the world was about to go to hell with us in it. Mama and Oma Haan never got along, although Mama tried her best, in her own words, to please Oma as best as she could. Mama said it was never enough anyhow. Oma had not been amused when her son married a woman with a 4-year-old child by "another man."

Mama was creative, beautiful, and had been an art designer for an advertising company when she worked in Amsterdam. She looked vibrant in her younger years, carefree as a teenager, and two older brothers to protect her. Nothing seemed out of the ordinary. She was a talented artist and accepted at the arts academy in her hometown. Then came Amsterdam, a great job, and an unexpected pregnancy, absolutely not accepted in those days. Mama had to return home to face her parents. Her Amsterdam dream was over fast, and I was born. Her young adult life stopped there. But my childhood stopped with that one statement from her in the car on our way home. From that singular moment on, I knew I had to take care of her.

3

— . —

THINGS ARE NOT AS THEY SEEM TO BE

Things are not as they seem to be

This was the second time she dropped a bomb on me. The first time was when I was eight. I was in my little room lying in my brand-new wooden box bed. Soon, I would move to the bigger bedroom, and my sister would be old enough to have mine. It might have been a restless night; it was late already. Maybe I had an argument with my dad that had sparked her initiative. Regardless of what made my mom come upstairs, things were about to change forever.

She sat down on the side of my bed and told me that my dad, the only paternal figure I had known, was not my real father. I had been adopted when they had met and decided to get married. But don't worry... He loved me endlessly... And this was true. He had done anything and everything to bring my childhood dreams to life. In Mama's story, he was amazing, strong-willed, and most of the time right (I couldn't help but smile at the admission). This saint chose me, and on and on. Emotional blackmail overload.

The subject was then never ever to be brought up again. I accepted it at that moment (what was I to do?), and we moved on. We—Mama, Dad, and I— agreed in some silent, secret pact to not bring it up again. However, only a few days later she *did* mention that my biological father lived in Amsterdam. They had met on a job, fallen in love, and she had me. Sweet, simple love story, right? Hardly. This prince was actually a married man with a string of kids, so Mama left Amsterdam and returned to her parents. Supposedly, my biological daddy-man had tried to reach out and see his baby. He even traveled all the way from Amsterdam to the other side of the country to see us. My grandpa, as the story goes, took the stuffed animal baby gift at the door, and sent him on his way, probably hoping the neighbors wouldn't notice.

So, after that night of stunning confessions and because the secret was out, Dad and I had frequent arguments, and of course, I thought I was always right. I had an arsenal of teenage wisdom. Arrogance overload. While I paid average attention in school, I acquired street knowledge available at a fast pace. Not sure the fact of him now being "only a stepdad" made it worse, but it just seemed to be the case. Now I was not only the perfect little girl, but surely "messed up forever" and with a secret no one could know about.

My sister had to be brought up to speed, as she was not aware of anything either, as I suddenly became her half-sister. We had more than 4 years between us, and as we grew up, that caused enough arguments. I only remember that I always screamed that she had gotten into my stuff. Not knowing if that was actually the case, I found enough reasons for upstairs war. Additionally, with this new knowledge of Dad-not-Dad, that made for more awkwardness between us, explaining all fights to be the cause of the fact that we were not the same. The truth was that my little sister was too young to comprehend, and meanwhile, I drowned myself in ballet classes and the attention of friends, my boyfriend, his seemingly "normal" family, sports, and meaningless high school drama. Our family dynamics were shattered forever but surely not noticeable. I just had to keep them underneath the surface.

I decided the best way to deal with all this homecrap and emotional overload on Mama's behalf was to become a popular teenage girl, and as the stage grew bigger, ballet gave me that confidence. Furthermore, my friends were the best friends in the world, with their superior wisdom and money that far surpassed mine. Surely, they had issues, at home, with school and with others. One of my girlfriend's mothers read her diaries, an absolutely unforgivable act of mistrust. Two other friends were raised by their single dads, but we never really thought that was a problem till the moment we were told 'no' to something we all wanted to do. Concerts, party gatherings at their house, movies, or travels. Parents' fault, what would they know? Observing their family troubles normalized mine and made me feel less alone. Overall, one would most likely say I was the "sunny girl," with the optimistic outlook and always dawning that "on" smile. I would try to mend arguments, heal wounds, and keep relationships afloat. The fixer of all things, that's who I was. Mother Goose, organizer of all rebel fun. Definitely on the road to rather helping others instead of digging into my own pain, or even acknowledging it. Surely, I would need adventure, fun, more fun, and a dance career like no other in order to forget about my troubles at home.

All that fun, though, could not overshadow how tense my relationship with my dad had become. I couldn't understand his black-and-white thinking, his rules and regulations, his blunt way of correcting me. He was not capable of showing me tender kindness and affection, unless I came home with awesome grades instead of drunk and cigarette smoking with friends on motorcycles, and I blamed him for lacking any communication skills whatsoever, he would *never* understand me.

On the other hand, I loved his sense of humor, endless affection, and love for my mother that he was able to show. His work ethic and relaxed manners around his friends and neighbors were comforting. As a high school teenager, I watched Archie Bunker because my dad did. I had a poster of the Partridge family above my bed, and even though he thought David Cassidy silly, he approved. Of course, I added a poster of Peter Frampton as well. I lived for dance, fashion, and pop music. ABBA won the Eurovision Song Contest in 1974, and my first LP albums were the musicals *Jesus Christ Superstar* and *Hair*. Thankfully these were accepted, as I was sold on Jesus. I guess that was my first sincere introduction to the life of Christ, as I could sing along and totally understand (in my innocent mind) what He was going through. Mama would sing all the lyrics of both musicals out loud while I danced through the house with her, and we would make Dad laugh. My wardrobe consisted of colorful India blouses and wide long skirts, flashy bright green flare corduroys and ugly pink V-neck sweaters. Oversized shirts combined with tight high waisted jeans, and not to forget the super high hippie platform clogs, mine were tri-color leather ones.

Not only did my mom support my musical abilities, but my love for fashion as well. She even signed me up to audition once for a fashion show. She had seen the announcement in the newspaper and wanted to expose me to the runway, more so because British actor Colin Baker, famous for playing Paul Merroney in the BBC television drama "The Hammonds," would make his appearance at this luxury department store, a sort of Dutch Neiman Marcus. Mama just had to have his autograph, so I got to strut the catwalk like a pro straight through the center of the store floor. My feet crossed according to what I remembered from television models, and my gray high heels matched my calf long ankle skirt with bright flowers and white top. I won the contest, 500 guilders cash (about $200) in prize money and a shopping spree for a few hundred more. I remember it like it was yesterday how Mama and I ravaged the upper floor filled with teenage clothing and makeup. And she did get her autograph.

To my surprise after my picture appeared in the newspaper (with actor Colin Baker and myself as Miss Lois Jeans 1976!), my high school life became a brief hell. Many groups, normally seen by "my gang" as unimportant and irrelevant, were now yelling and whistling at me in front of the doors of the bicycle stalls and hallways. For months, I endured makeup and fashion jokes, modeling wannabe remarks and mimed runway struts in front of me by other kids, legs crossed and sarcastic attitudes. It was stupid teenage hell that led to me go home crying rivers. Yet, Mama was still proud and had all the right answers.

"Don't bother with them. Chin up, stay your path, and believe in yourself," she would say. She gave me the endless powers of self-esteem and determination although I would not realize that until years later.

Dad didn't say much, as he never did, but years later Mama told me that he was seen running through the streets telling the neighbor I won. He was so proud and excited. He just never showed or verbalized it to me.

But at school, all I wanted was to escape and hang with the coolest kids, and one day I got invited to this party in the attic of this student's house. It was Christmas. I was 16 and fell for this nice boy hard and fast. Finally, a great group to belong to, by choice, cool rich kids with motorcycles and in my eyes, all the freedom they wanted. I had the courage to introduce my high school boyfriend to my parents, and from then on, he would be the one to save me from my ever-more-drinking mother and my difficult father who would never understand me anyway. From this point on, you'll know him as Mr. First.

4

— · —

SEEMINGLY HAPPY YEARS

When I was very little, my mother had instilled in me the silly, yet lasting thought that I was a princess sent off to the normal peasants for adoption because living an ordinary life would serve my royal responsibilities later. I believed it to be as real as Santa Claus. *Ugh, what the heck was she thinking? How would this type of princess tale grant me a better understanding of the world?*

"Don't forget; you are special," Mama would say.

She would always laugh and squeeze me to pieces. I gracefully tippy toed around the house, making an appearance as a superstar in every room, performing for my family and friends. I was cute. "Sunshine child," they called me. I always danced, and I was Grandpa's darling. I lived mainly for compliments and hugs. Oh, how cute must I have been with those big eyes.

I also remember vividly, at about 12 years old, visiting the outdoors Saturday morning farmers market in town with a girlfriend. A man behind the fruit stand told me that I had "porn" eyes.

"You should be happy about it," he laughed. "I'm sure that you'll get lots of work."

Fucker. What a dick. I honestly had no idea what he meant at that time, but I knew it was rude and uncalled for. I told my mom, crying when I came home, and she went ballistic, furious, ready to take that market guy down. Moments like these became more common as I aged, each one freaking me out more than the one before.

Something deep inside of me wanted to be more than pretty. I wanted and needed to be called smart. But I was not smart and made it through high school on just above average scores. Maybe I could have done a lot better on my intelligence merits, but it was more important to me to gather up with the gang of friends than to pay too much attention to homework. In my eyes, I needed to be there for everyone and everything, and, I must admit, the gang did lots of awesome, cool stuff.

My life-long, lasting love for dance started when a beautiful lady opened a ballet class in our little town. She moved in next door above the stables of the farmhouse facing our home, and she immediately started gathering a few pink-dressed little girls in her living room to teach them how to dance. She had come from far away, was in our eyes a famous ex-ballerina with a huge career. Although I never knew the truth, or where she came from, she appeared as an angel to me, and instilled in me the love for dance.

I was maybe 8 or 9 years old, and my fellow dance friends and I were quickly moved to the local library. That same library some days served as a church, some days as a dance studio, and sometimes hosted important town halls. Mama was still healthy, thin, beautiful, and popular amongst the other mothers, and would host events with the other moms across from the dance classes filled with other twinkling girls.

I loved and adored Ms. Bee, as I felt seen and admired by her. She made me feel music, feel my body breathe, feel my emotions. She made us move to music and experience the amazing capabilities of our muscles, and what our bodies could do, and what movement could bring up in other people, emotionally. We had annual ballet performances at the local hotel and bar across from the library, which served as a public event room since it had a large stage. Everyone would come out to see us. My first tutu hung down like a round, layered circle, and Mama had to start all over again, as all the mothers would make new costumes for each event. It was a huge event, and I could shine more than I ever wanted, center stage. Ms. Bee had it made in our town with the ballet troupe, and she was adored by all. And by one gentleman, a little too much.

Our sweet friend's father left her mother for Ms. Bee! The news shocked and devastated all of us. As the new couple "fled to America," the huge scandal exploded through our small town. She moved so far away, without a note nor little warning. So there I was, an 11-year-old girl in a pink ballet leotard. Less than innocent, I tried to comprehend that "stuff" about sex. *Was it true?* Gossip must be real and even the most adored and admired people around us are not so holy at all. Secrecy amongst the adults left us girls heartbroken, and my parents had to reassure me constantly that they were happy together and that neither would run away with someone else.

I was devastated and in no mood to take any other adult seriously, ever again. It didn't help that my parents started attending and hosting parties during the same time. I was not amused, and in my eyes, it was super embarrassing. Their not-so-adult boisterous and joyful behavior, framed by Bacharach and Beatles music, would get louder and louder at night. So did the voices of excitement and gossip with lots of people sitting *way* too close to each other on our new, totally hip, low back brown couch. Not to mention that all my "aunties" and "uncles" could be seen (and heard) dancing around the floors of the living room and kitchen in the wee hours of the morning. We had an open staircase (in those days awesome never-heard-of modern and far out top design), dark brown wood, in the middle of the living room going upstairs to the first floor.

During those parties, I would lay flat on the floor of the upstairs hallway, drop my head slightly over the last stairwell, and peek between the open spaces at the wild but attractive mess that happened in our house. So significant, that this staircase that opened my eyes to the world, would be the same staircase that later took my dad's life in a gruesome way.

Alcohol turned it all upside down. Slowly. As a teenager, in my case. You don't want to see it at first, then you deny it, then you hide it from others, then it becomes public knowledge and then just accepted.

What the heck happened? Nobody stepped in? Could any-one help my mom? Was I the only one that was trying, now daily, to keep her alert, attentive, and in the moment? Trying to lift her up? More concerning, my four years younger sister was still at home when I left for Amsterdam, and I was concerned about her. We would hardly communicate but pretended to keep the fun going, as the perfect family dream that still lived inside us. I loved my parents and sister so much and loved my childhood years. But how in the world were we able to endure these episodes of family loss, intense grief, and drunkenness, while still pretending everything was great?

My boyfriend's home was my safe place. His mother, Joosje, was a busy and caring working woman. She had a career in education, and educated the heck out of me, or better said, in me. She gave constant advice on how to improve myself, to surround myself with people that are better educated, to challenge myself, to dress for the future, to go to university, to do the best I could, and so forth. My place was there, where I was reminded of my abilities, my skill set, my gifts and talents, reminded to never give up and move on.

I did not realize, at that time, that she was not able to show warm, kind, and embracing love like my mom did. That's why Mr. First was drawn to my mother so much, he absolutely loved my hugging and loving mother. And again, we didn't discuss my inability to help my alcoholic mom. Our mothers had become friends, and my now second mom knew, of course, what I faced in my house and took me under her wing as a daughter. She had three sons, so I was a welcome breath of air.

Joosje, boyfriend's mother, had the time and energy to teach me about life, wardrobes, careers, silverware and table settings, sewing, savings, and sharing. Always overdress, not underdress, for any occasion. Show up for success. Show style and grace. She taught me about gardening and cooking, although I bailed mostly on those two when needed. But I would clean up, and oh my, did I always scrub. I still do. I believe cleaning and scrubbing has saved me from disasters many times. One of my coping mechanisms is cleaning, folding, and putting things away. Still, when I feel down, I clean. It gives me time to think, stay busy, and feel accomplished. As long as I keep moving. The alternative is sitting down and drinking. Or getting caught up in some other behavioral mishap. Addictive behavior runs in the family, runs in many families as I have learned over the years.

Sometimes my friends and I would wonder how we were being perceived, throughout high school, university years, business years. Our image, my image, thinking about ourselves, how we would come across, in general, is something that during our upbringing never came up. In our Dutch world, thinking about yourself was not necessarily a thing. People would serve others and besides that, people would just live their lives. The old Protestant way of life kept us modest. Don't stand out! Fit in!

Being greedy is not necessary. Just be, that's more than enough.

Sometimes people would call me exotic, funny, or unique. I started thinking about that more and more, as in search of the meaning of those statements from others. Though, still bothersome, I would wonder what in the world does that mean? What am I going to do with these descriptions? That's not me, for sure! I am far from exotic! Funny maybe, I do love to dress up, or try something new, just being my silly self.

But I was also without a real father, and I had a drunk mother. I was a poor princess, not really belonging and without belongings!

5

— • —

DISCO REBEL

THEN I GET NIGHT FEVER, NIGHT FEVER, WE KNOW HOW TO DO IT GIMME THAT NIGHT FEVER, NIGHT FEVER, WE KNOW HOW TO SHOW IT   ~BEE GEES, "NIGHT FEVER"

As much as I have danced to the waves of these disco songs, I can't tell but I believe it was a true blessing to be young in the disco era. The lights, the moves, the discotheque, my girlfriends, and I loved it and could dance for hours, the happy music, the sexy tunes. We didn't visit many in town, but I remember two establishments that truly reflected the padded walls and the disco balls. This fun retro interior design of Studio 54. And that was big.

Dance was still my escape, probably my most important escape throughout my entire life. (Coping mechanism, if you will.) I believe now, in the present day, that dancing saved me. As my research and speaking engagements teach, dance and movement are a constant and proven successful way to process trauma, loss, and hardship. Trauma and pain are facts of life, but we know that trauma reshapes our brain and will manifest in our body. Movement is healing, and healing can start with movement, with any form of dance. I was not aware of that in those days, nor did I know then that my story would serve my purpose towards helping others.

At about 16, I started going to high school parties, must-see-concerts, and can't-miss disco gatherings at all the best places in town myself. On the square, at the most popular bar, you could find us, the gang, just hanging out. Trying awkward, questionable, colorful, and cheap liquor shots. How we made it home safely, I have no clue. We did everything on motorcycles, I was always hanging on in the seat behind my boyfriend's backside, stuffed into thick leather coats and helmets. We would even drive the bike to take dance lessons learning the foxtrot and the waltz together, with my silver dance shoes packed in a bag and my long skirt waving in the wind.

I thought I had landed in heaven, with such an amazing group of loyal best friends, especially since I preferred to be at their homes with their seemingly perfect parents. We truly enjoyed the beauty and environment around my boyfriend's house, where we could walk the endless woods and pastures surrounding their home.

Knowing as well that by this time, my high school years, I could find my mom drunk, and she would embarrass the heck out of me. At home I did not feel popular; the emotions were now always loaded. Mama would be tipsy, and Dad would be mad at me because he was maybe mad at her. Or maybe just mad at me? Even though he did his utmost best to be a just and responsible dad, the tension between us grew thicker and thicker. Now, so many years later, I know that he must have felt so confused, not being able to understand what my mom was going through. It really started to get worse when my uncle died, and then shortly after, my grandma. She could not handle the loss and grief, I believe. And Dad was not raised in a household that talked about feelings, loss, emotions, pain.

Through our dysfunction, I found my light at the end of the tunnel. Either the bright lights of the disco establishments or the dimmed lights of the dance academy—a huge, stone dark building with large ballet floors and bars, classes in ballet and character dance which is a specific subcategory of classical dance representing a stylized traditional folk or national European dance. This school would set the preparation for an eventual step to the real deal. Academy preschool was set to make or break you, and expectations were high.

At this school, I would meet two lifetime friends, and from then on, their homes were sanctuaries as well, especially since we would enter the Friday night disco together, glued to the dance floor in a three sum till midnight. Roosmarie had beautiful long, brown hair, and she had a strong, huge personality. We were both driven and obsessed with dance and ballet and convinced we were the next best thing that Amsterdam needed. Our dance brother, Roel, the first homosexual friend I had, was my high school bestie, and I had told him about the opportunity to join this pre-academy. I knew he loved to dance, and I was somewhat protective of him at times my fellow high school students would give him hell. Now the three of us were a pact, bonded by our love for dance, convinced we could dance forever. The disco became our permanent stage, as the movie *Saturday Night Fever* made its entrance, and the dance moves became second nature. We showed off our moves after long evenings in our room deciding what to wear and how to get there.

Mama would drive during the week, and my supportive and caring dad, if he and I would not argue, was the one who drove me on Saturdays to pre-training for dance academy. An hour drive, Tuesdays, Thursdays, and Saturdays, during my last two high school years—*Whew!* It called for such commitment, but I knew that it was worth it.

Rigorous training sessions, girls in pink leotards and one young man prepared to audition for the real deal. Ultimately, being chosen to train at a real dance academy (there were only three in the country) was a huge deal. And one must prepare. I had been dancing since I was four and convinced my parents during my last year in high school that there was no alternative to dance and ballet. Dad did, ultimately, not agree and clearly stated I would not have anything to fall back on when I break a leg. On top of that, with my back I wouldn't stand a chance to make it in the world of dance.

No career options, no chance to make money. *Not with my bad Notre Dame hunchback!*

6

— · —

THERE ARE SHORTCUTS TO HAPPINESS

D ancing is one of them.

My right shoulder is much higher than the left, and thus my front rib cage on the left sticks out more than the right side. It looks and feels like I carry a backpack on the right side only. I have to correct it constantly, till the day I die, but by doing so I hope I can prevent it from getting worse over time. Others don't notice, but I think they do. A beautiful, low back bathing suit is out of the question. So are beautiful bras and tailor-made *Victoria Secret* lingerie. They just don't fit.

I was born with scoliosis and not a small case. Cute girl with huge blue eyes and a damaged body image. My mother had ignored doctors with wheelchair predictions and horror stories about scoliosis (deformed people) and decided that ballet was the only way to correct my posture and that that would be good for me. As advised, she made me frequently walk around with a book on my head. Bless Mama for those life-altering decisions. It was decided; movement over surgery.

Little did she know that my scoliosis would set the stage for my back-trauma as well as the stage for my successful fitness future. She told me as well that I had no waist and no butt because of my deformed spine. I am not talking about wanting more, but looking like a matchbox, in my mom's words, was something to be grateful about. Not fun though because later in life I really wanted to have a round butt, a size zero, Dolly Parton waist and somewhat of a real boob deal. Not my AAA cup size. You are of an "athletic build," they would say, but I didn't understand that could be handy later in life.

My days were soon filled with walking around with books on my head thanks to Ms. Bee. She saved me. Dancing a few times a week brought me to life like nothing else. Like I said, it felt so free, liberating, creative, and beautiful. My thing was ballet. I was going to go through with it no matter what people would say about my ugly back. Ms. Bee had been not just an amazing teacher, she was making me feel beautiful as well, teaching and sharing with me ways to physically adjust my scoliosis so that I had the ability to dance and feel like any other 8-year-old girl.

In an attempt to cheer us young dance friends up and continue our prima ballerina careers, a few parents had found an arts academy, a decent school where the ballet class was run by a male teacher. This may be a relief after knowing that women can run off with husbands. Oh my, we were blown away. By God, this man looked like a Greek statue, muscles everywhere, handsome, tall and blond, and it didn't help that he was nice as well and recognized our talents, and of course, as special as we were in our minds, started an advanced ballet class for just us, a few of the chosen. For me!

Amazing teacher, Bert, made me work harder, be more disciplined, and realize that I had to fight my body, my handicap. He praised my beautiful arms and my endlessly long legs and told me they were worth a million bucks. Of course, my legs were endlessly long, I did not have an upper body, remember? Glad, at least, that these extremities were working for me—and my big blue eyes. I was in ballet heaven again while our parents took turns driving us those weeks to this school which was not close by either. I realized how amazing our parents were to take on this enterprise. Finally, we were a great group again—a few of the girls from my small town and a few other girls. One of these girls was beautiful, exotic, and named Dolores.

The next summer, a few of us were invited to stay on a campground with Bert and his wife, who we knew and trusted at this point. The parents were comfortable with this idea as well and dropped us off for a few days, camping and running around outdoors with our amazing handsome teacher and his family—a fabulous vacation. I don't remember much but can still feel and picture the shape of our little tent and smell the wet grass in front of it. I remember us playing Santana all day and dancing to the music in front of our tents. Once back home, all I knew, as I can still feel the intense pain, was our classes were canceled. I had no idea what happened, no words, no explanations. Bert was far away, his sweet wife was in shock and crying, and the beautiful girl and minor—I don't believe she was even 16 years old—Dolores had gone with him.

When my high school years started, I was in pre-academy in town. I met beautiful Rosemarie and Roel, who both became a major influence for me to not give up. We were able to dance the weekends nights away when I was staying with them in town, while on weekdays and Saturday mornings we put on our toe shoes, leotards and worked our bodies in a sweat for hours and hours. That was our pledge together, the start of a promise to each other to dance through life. To dance our fears, our anger, our frustration away. The start of a long struggle to hide my scoliosis and prove myself.

Because I never knew why or had answers, I made up my own stories. To talk about alcohol and drug abuse was not really done in those days. My first love quickly became my salvation. He was going to be my forever, he, and his amazing family. His loving mother became my second mom, and she reminded me that this princess is going to have the love affair of the century. She was wrong because I became a weeping hopeless baby when he fell for someone else in high school.

I did everything I could to get him back. I fought, cried rivers, wrote notes, and he came back. I was in charge, having to prove myself because I felt abandoned by my parents and would not approve this to happen again. Looking back, I probably behaved like a ridiculous teenager desperate for attention. According to me, my boyfriend had to be with me, as well as our circle of friends. These friendships were everything and had to continue, at all costs. I would go to any length for them. My teenage years started with my boyfriend, his family, and great high school friends that are still around as of today, and fun years of travel and high school adventures.

7

PRINCESS WITHOUT A PEA

It was an impersonal room. Just a bed and a nightstand with a backdrop of gray walls. It smelled like a pingy hospital. The aroma of medication and bath salts made me want to pinch my nose. Dad's short description was probably accurate, as he was trying to explain her voluntary rehab facility to me, and besides the above explanation, he said it was going to be alright.

The rehab sanatorium became my mom's new home. I couldn't blame my dad for becoming so hopeless at helping her. He really had no other choice.

I was still at home and in high school, and Mama's daily drinking became impossible. That and a daily dose of medication, rather a surplus of benzos (or Benzodiazepine, a depressant) and other medication daily consumed and eternally refilled by our family physician (who had an open-door policy when it comes to my mother). They were "best friends," after all. Mama started reading early '70s Sartre's work on existentialism and Thomas Harris's famous book, *I'm Okay, You're Okay*. She increasingly questioned her life and possibilities, feeding her depression and adding on more confusion. Possibilities to seek help somewhere else were unknown to us, and I had no clue such places even existed. Dad told my sister and I that Mama would be on a short "retreat" vacation to find herself, but shortly after, he would confess it was an alcohol recovery treatment facility. At this time, detox clinics were not common, so I could not imagine what that had to do with Betty Ford

I knew and could feel that he was hopeful something or someone would be able to help her. It turned out to be a joke, in my mom's words, as she came home after three days. I don't even know where she went; I just remember that she said that all the counselors and psychiatrists and therapists loved her and would all spend hours telling her their life stories.

"Nobody listened to me," she said laughing aloud. "They all wanted to talk to me instead."

Not surprising, since that was her endless role. Loving, caring, and intelligent, she would turn the tables. End of story. End of any possibility of seeking outside help. Back to our status quo, as where my dad finally just decided to join my mother in her quest for alcohol and started drinking at the same tempo and probably the same amount as Mama. For a long time, Mama did try; they both did. Their next collaborative effort was that Mama was going to work. A part-time job would support her transition to sobriety. She got a job at the factory where Dad worked, and they drove together. Mama was there for half days and then home when my sister and I returned after school, and this routine continued for a few years, and things at home seemed to be under control. Mama lost weight, was happy. There was less stress and lots of laughter, especially when she'd tell us stories about the ladies at her workplace, the people they now both knew, and the five o'clock happy hour drink called *borrel*, a shot of Dutch Jenever. *Tijd voor een borreltje* (time for a drink) was the daily sign. The term "functional alcoholic" had not been introduced to us yet.

During this time, I graduated high school, but my sister still had years to go at home. She must have been really fed up with our parents and in a hurry to graduate and leave. She was increasingly ignored, became silent, stayed in her room, left to visit friends, and stayed away from people who would visit the house. There was lots of laughter and friendship at our house, sweet family members and other parents living in town coming to visit. But there was drinking involved, now on every occasion. Louder, earlier in the day and more frequent, each party became more obnoxious. By all involved, my sister was considered very creative but introverted, and everyone accepted that label. I guess she had no choice, either.

That was obviously, according to every visitor knowing best, the reason why she would mainly stay in her room. What a web of lies we lived. Meanwhile, since I had moved out and my sister would not care anymore, I phoned and listened daily to my drunk mom.

Sometimes I shared my stories about my brand-new life at the dance academy and my adventures in Amsterdam. About my room, roommates, joining a garage band with no rock future, dance dreams and late-night disco outings. No clue what my sister was doing, I failed to show interest in her and her teenage life. I was mostly super annoyed with Mama. I hardly talked to Dad during that time. It seemed he worked all the time and now started to drink with her when home. It all felt so out of sorts, far away, disconnected from my loved ones at home—the house and neighborhood I loved. I could not communicate with Mama and was afraid Dad would not approve of anything I said, suggested, or tried.

About two years after moving to Amsterdam, in another attempt to find myself, I started a search for my biological father. Mama had told me his name and that he was an artist and graphic designer. He even had his commercials on the television. Still, I had no idea where he had been the last 20 years, and at home it was never mentioned. Of course, there was no Google or cell phones like today. I only had the yellow pages, so I started with that and looked for his last name. It didn't take a long time since I knew he had been a big name in the design and advertising industry, a sector that I could find combing through the business pages. His advertising agency was actually listed and still located in Amsterdam.

I remember calling. He was quiet when I introduced myself as his daughter. I explained that I was curious to meet him. After a few minutes into the conversation, he seemed excited to meet me and suggested a coffee in a city restaurant. I was shaking, nervous and anxious. Our first meeting led to a few others, all over cups of coffee. I liked him, looked somewhat like him, and I saw what I needed to see. He was jovial, had a great sense of humor and was talented, creative. A great writer. He loved jazz music and the outdoors. Sadly, our relationship didn't develop. It fizzled away into occasional calls and then just died. His wife at the time was not a fan after she found out, and that made it even more uncomfortable. She had a daughter that was their number one. He also had a few other kids. Oh well, I let it go.

Not sure why I discussed this at first sight during a successful (considering our history) but still rather disappointing adventure with Mama, but of course, she told Dad. This move closed the door on our relationship forever. The fact that I had searched for acceptance and love elsewhere hurt him so badly that he called me and asked what kind of nonsense I was up to, not understanding why I had the nerve to dishonor him and disgrace our family. We didn't see eye-to-eye for years to come and hardly spoke to each for months.

8

— · —

DANCE ACADEMY & STAGE

A few pieces of clothing would do although I always made work of my wardrobe. As I had made it a point to be a trendsetter in high school, wearing purple and apple green corduroy flare pants, bright orange and pink woolen sweaters, combined with days of oversized white shirts from my dad, long skirts, a tricolor woolen scarf and penny loafers. Hippy snob, preppy, relaxed. High heels or boots. Nothing else would be necessary for my life in Amsterdam as any other fashion trend I followed was readily available right there. And I knew I would spend most of my days in black leotards and pink tights, the standard ballet uniform. My blue canvas bag filled up quickly with two pairs of pointe shoes on top.

I left for Amsterdam after I graduated, a year before my boyfriend and most of my friends in the gang. They had another year to go, because they did a Gymnasium or Atheneum level of education, preparation for scientific studies in the Netherlands, a level of higher education and then I chose, or rather was pointed out to follow. Nevertheless, I had, in my eyes, a great education and even greater high school years. This was due to my cool gang of friends who had stuck by me and were now endlessly aware and forgiving towards my mom and my circumstances.

We all knew things, secrets we had shared and seen about our parents, about our families, now somewhat accepted and talked about—or ignored, as teenagers do. Because now we were 18 and knew better. We knew it all. We were about to show and conquer the world out there. We had the world by the tail. I was going to the big city. Most of my high school peers would join other cities, with more popular universities, or would stay close to the place they were born and join trade schools or stay on the farm. That year I was the only one going to Amsterdam. Roosmarie, my only friend to join me, was my bestie from the pre-formative dance academy.

I chose to go through the awful process of auditioning for the Dance Academy in Arnhem and Amsterdam. Arnhem was a backup in case I was rejected. The process of auditioning is not nice, and of course, they would bring up the fact that I might not be able to dance professionally because of my handicap—my ugly scoliosis back. But, according to the voices in charge at that moment, I did have talent, was very well trained, and certainly could look forward to a long life of dance and teaching.

I took it as an insult, but realized it was the truth. I was never going to look good on stage or fit in a troupe of perfectly equal looking swans or play the back row swan forever. Dad thought it was not a good pick, but Mama knew my passion and my heart's desire better than anyone else. So, yes, I won. Off to the big city of Amsterdam and off to a tough, challenging and physically demanding daily dance academy.

The dance academy brought me to life. Away from home, away from the constant worry about Mama's health. I quickly make new friends, with the same dreams as I had. My boyfriend and I stayed together, awaiting the day that he would be able to join me in Amsterdam to study international law. When I left high school, he had joined the military for an 18-month commitment. So, I went into this adventure alone, without the security of backup, family, his mother, and high school buddies. Mama dropped me off after we found a room for rent in just one weekend. The stars felt like they were aligning.

It was a dark, small, and depressing room, in an apartment on the third floor. The entire apartment smelled like the old lady that lived there. She had a toilet but no shower, which was not uncommon at the time, as a bath house was available in every street. And according to Mama, I could spend hours in the showers at the dance academy since we would take many showers a day anyway. In my new room was a bed, a chest, a chair, and as many crosses of Jesus Christ on the wall that you could think of. It was a decoration thing. He always stared at me.

Not that I didn't love Jesus, but there was way too much of him making me feel small, unworthy, and guilty of all sin in the world. My journey was not going to start like this, too creepy. When I would ask to use her rotary phone to call home, she would sit right next to me and give me a deep sigh after a minute, as if it was going to cost her a fortune if I stayed on it any longer. Creepy indeed. I feared her and her many Jesuses. Use of the toilet increasingly caused her to sigh and frown, and the kitchen and refrigerator stayed off limits.

My mind was made up in no time—this place was not permanent, and I had to look for something else immediately. Finding a place that was close to the school with public transportation was not an easy thing to do in a busy city. This address was convenient and easy to find. I was living in the southside of the city, which, according to my mom, was the more upscale Jewish part of town. I do vividly remember that a small window gave the room some light, and at night the lights from the busy street below would give me some comfort. At least I had company in the deep dark night.

At night I felt present, somewhat excited, scared, and super aware all at the same time. Adjusting to the noise that resonated from the big city, I remember listening to the endlessly moving trams and buses and the night owls that would step out drunk to stumble their way home. The city reeked of smoke, gasoline, and warm fresh baked bread all at the same time. There were bells, birds, hums, pops, cats, dogs, audible and inaudible, soft, and loud, keeping me up for hours before I would drift off, already exhausted from the new impressions and demands of the academy and my new life.

Only after a few months, I moved into another tiny place, creeped out by the demands of my landlady and her Holy Moly. I found another landlady in the same neighborhood with a slightly larger apartment, right under the rooftop away from the owners that lived two stories below. It had two very small rooms—one that could fit a bed and was attached by a tiny corridor with a shelf that served as kitchen. I thought it was huge, and I was in heaven.

My separate living room was decorated by Ikea with a real couch and table and my 21-inch television. And plants. Lots of them. They brought life back to mine. A brother and sister team moved in next door, in another two attic-turned-into-living-quarters spaces. They quickly became my new friends. They were deeply devout Christians and introduced me to Jesus in an entirely different way. At that time, I was not verbal or comfortable about my spiritual beliefs or upbringing. After being invited to my first ever church camp week, I knew more songs, games, prayers, and lots of kumbaya things I had not experienced before.

Wow, everyone was so friendly and kind, and always so happy! Now that I was closer to God, spiritually more than physically (without creepy crosses all over the walls), I was convinced that I would walk in Jesus' own footsteps and change the world.

The ballet days were physically demanding, and the expectations increased. We had sweet but tough teachers, all seniors in the business, with expired or early ending careers as performers who taught us the grinds and hardships of being a dancer. I made friends, and some turned into friends for life. (Not a week goes by we don't talk, even all these years later separated by an entire ocean). On weekends we would hang out in the Kandinsky Theater watching movies with Rudolf Nureyev or Mikhail Baryshnikov, giggling and being in love with such amazing dancers. My toe shoes would hang out of my bag on the way to school in the morning on the early tram. Anyone would see I was a dancer—my feet turned 180 degrees when walking, upright and proud. I was going to change the world, remember? And I shall do it with dance and movement. Anyone could feel as empowered as I was in those early mornings. I always loved the mornings in the city.

When in school, I worked my butt off trying to fit in with my awful looking back and in my eyes, malformed body. I was respected and loved, but every so often, during a class, I would feel dismayed. The looks I received during rehearsals for an in-house performance coming up...I didn't fit in, and I knew it. And at the same time, not aware yet of the dire consequences, dinners became wine and cigarettes in a desperate attempt to stay at or under the required weight. My newly gained friends and I all went through the same, listening to sentimental songs and Motown beats, dancing in our apartments and rehearsing choreography, but scared to eat.

We loved chocolate bars and oranges, cigarettes to suppress hunger and wine to fill our bellies. Student life. At night I would throw up, feeling so guilty about eating, getting rid of all foods that had entered my body. It could have been the alcohol as well, although I don't remember drinking too much. That was not an option with a ballet class at 8 am. Nevertheless, it was an early start for an addictive mind with an onset of anorexia that would last a lifetime.

It was also popular to be a size zero, skinny as a rail. We started mornings at the academy being weighed in on a scale and pinched in our upper arms with a weird looking piece of equipment that would measure our fat content. It was an ancient body mass index tool. Pure abuse in my eyes, but, of course, was considered a fairly normal part of our daily procedures. Much of the academy culture, as I look back at it now, would not be considered a healthy mental, emotional, and physical environment. My hair was pulled back so tightly, and I still wear it daily in the same fashion now because I don't know the difference. Believing my grandma tales, maybe because I hope that way my face stays lifted, and I am not getting older. But I forgot about my neck, darn it, as it shows many chins and wrinkles, and now you can certainly tell I am not 39 anymore, which is a hopeless feeling.

I hate getting older, physically that is. I struggle with the fact that I cannot dance anymore, that my chronic pain is increasing as I age, that I cannot work out like a maniac anymore, something I love to do. Shoot, only ten years ago I opened a studio and was able to teach four or five classes a day, of which at least one or two were high-impact boxing or strength classes. I loved it so much but might be suffering from the professional fitness-person imposter syndrome and falling apart because I did too much. How would you be able to tell? It is a catch-22. The professional does it all but does not know her own physical limitations.

No wonder I became an anorexic without realizing the lifelong impact. Most of us probably walked away from those years with an eating disorder. As of today, I have an unhealthy relationship with food, don't like preparing it, and most times love dining out. I eat to live and do not live to eat. It is not something to be discussed with others, that would put me on the spot, and I always avoid that. Talking about myself is not my best attribute, mostly because nobody is asking, and I don't feel it makes any sense. Reaching out is not something I did or do, as in not asking for empathy, sympathy, understanding, or help. Not because I don't want to, or make attempts to, but I just don't know how.

How many times at work or in a social setting did I try and fail? I opened up, but when one came emotionally too close for comfort, I pulled back or completely withdrew. I left so many times, moved so many times, always scared of allowing someone in. If I let them in, they will also leave me. Abandonment issues for life. And maybe because people see me as being different, most friends nor family never asked anything personally. It becomes a lonely path. For that matter, my eating disorder became undiscussed, a path of trying some diets, nutrition tips, the occasional health trips, and years of not caring what I would eat.

Nowadays, becoming increasingly aware of the past pains and a slow understanding of where I find myself, my loving partner and I have decided that we both eat to live.

I still have a love–hate relationship with food, love to go out for dinner and hate to cook. Our grocery list is plain, simple, and mostly the same, but very decent on the "what is healthy" scale. Finally, I appreciate life, to the fullest, and be conscious of the fact that I would like to live another twenty years. My friend, an amazing author, nationally known nutrition speaker, and wellness educator, taught me much over the years we traveled together as presenters at conventions. I would attend her sessions and become aware of a better, healthier lifestyle I could easily adjust to. Even repeating the phrase, "If you don't take care of your body, where are you going to live?"

I stayed at the academy for two years and then left the school. I had great fun and exciting experiences, worked on amazing choreographies and performances, learned the hardship of pointe shoe classes. I spent hours in movement a day, from the first classical class in the morning to contemporary, jazz, tap and Spanish dance classes. Hours of rigorous exercise combined with a mixture of sessions of dance notation, anatomy, and music was all part of my first experiences with discipline and determination. I became simultaneously determined and more insecure at the academy as time progressed. Add to that, being constantly judged and in a constant mode of competition with classmates, and one very inappropriate evening with the music teacher drove me further in doubt.

All I remember is him coming over to my tiny two-room attic, with a mission regarding the music class that day. I needed tutoring, or he needed my notes, why else would he visit my apartment? While on my small couch, he started leaning over while I sat on the floor. In no time he was on top of me, ready to play in a way I could never imagine. He started to touch me, fondle, my breast and legs, caressing. I did say stop. I did say no. When I started to push and fight, he released me. He asked me not to bring it up, apologized and left immediately.

As startled and upset I was, I didn't feel I could mention it to anyone. It felt stupid and made me feel utterly inferior. I thought academy leadership would not understand since it happened in my tiny room. How could I ever explain he was there for academic reasons, improving my understanding of the curriculum? He was taking an interest in my notes? On top of that, I lived in a world of body awareness and physical touch. For us ballerinas, it was normal to touch and be touched all day, by each other and teachers. Not inappropriately but as part of the profession. Corrections were physical; dress rehearsals and costume tryouts were physical; consequences were physical; injuries and physical therapists were physical.

Feeling disturbed, confused, and shocked, I dropped the thoughts of the event, suppressed it, and tried to act some-what normal in his sessions. For me, that's where a huge disconnect with my physical self-started. As if my body was part of me, but without emotional connection with it. I never mentioned that teacher incident, until now. I was ashamed, guilty-ridden, and alone. More physical abuse would follow. Funny how I fit right in with the #MeToo movement, even though 40 years after the first incident.

About two years later, a similar situation occurred.

For the first time ever, it felt like a university professor viewed me as smart and competent. For the first time, I thought a professor took me seriously. For the first time, I wasn't only beautiful, but I was also smart.

Not only did he seem to admire my intellect, but the feelings were mutual as I purposefully sat in the first row of his lectures. I could not get enough of his philosophy class and promised him some project notes afterwards. Not realizing if or when he needed them, till one day he invited me over to his house.

Unaware and innocent maybe, he had a nice hot bath running and asked me to take a bath with him. He said he wanted me. In an instinctual reflex, I knew to run. He never saw me in the audience again. I was so disgusted, scared, and angry. Afraid to tell my boyfriend. Afraid to discuss the proposal. More afraid I would get the blame. Huh, I was pretty, nicely dressed on average days, sometimes loved the teacher's attention and took the bait. Naive and stupid.

Did I feel naive afterwards? In retrospect, I had this conversation with God many times then and over the course of my life. Who is to blame? Are men just attracted to body parts and women more contextually dependent? Was I leading anybody on? I was not but had and still have a tendency to look at man, somewhat naively. As if they were always friendly friends and without intentions of lust, sexuality, or desire. Of course, I dressed up and could be desirable. But I was not at all provocative. In general, I believe women dress up for other women, not to seduce men.

During the second year, the Ballet Academy teachers told me that they really wanted to work with me. They loved my drive and performance. I made progress, but they probably had me repeat the year to see if I could continue to improve with my scoliosis. I only heard what I would hear over and over in the future, what became unwanted, the repetitive story of my life. *You are different and awesome, but we don't know what to do with you. You are so talented, great poise and posture, love your energy, beautiful lines, great execution, but your back is a problem.* Blah blah blah.

I was scared to fail, not feeling accepted, not being able to fulfill expectations of family, friends, and teachers, and mostly tired of their judgment. It was the first time that I made a decision on my own, knowing that failing the dance academy was not really an option. I probably left a day before they could tear me down, fail me and repeat the year. My best friends at the time stayed but were loyal to my decisions. As usual, I was terrified of failure and terrified to fail my dad, so I had to make amends and find a more exciting and pleasing alternative. I was alone and had to make choices.

And of course, it had to be more exciting, as I now realize that everything always had to be more interesting than any venture I had taken on before. I had to prove them wrong. I could dance. As much as I wanted to. To make a solid splash for my parents and immediate loved ones, and hopefully a much-appreciated move, I joined the University of Amsterdam with a major in Art History and Archeology and a minor in pedagogy and psychology to appease my dad and live up to everyone else's expectations. I was curious and excited.

Dad expressed it was *onnodig*—an unnecessary move—especially since a large part of my education was paid for by scholarships from the company he worked for. I should have tried harder, not given up, and stayed at the academy. Retake the second ballet year if that was what they wanted. But I was going to prove my dad wrong. I could still be a dancer with a company that showed interest in me, and I would study at a real university! How pleasing is that, and it sounds good! I was going to study to fit in and succeed in something, even if it was considered a fun major, with a curriculum that Dad considered to be kind of weak. Stubborn to follow my instincts, madly driven by the ballet company's unfair treatment, and not being understood, I had signed up for university, and took two (in my eyes) gigantic exams in mathematics to be eligible. My weakest class in high school had been math, even after countless evenings with Dad who was a superstar with numbers and mentored me. I passed on my own merit, and Dad was very proud.

This accomplishment brought about much joy for me. My boyfriend and I would finally be together again in Amsterdam as he studied law, and I joined a jazz dance performance company. Things were looking up and I could not wait to begin this new promising adventure.

9

ADULTING SUCKS

Mr. First was an easy roommate. We made our way together in our single-wide mobile home behind a rose nursery farmstead. A beautiful setting. We fixed it up and painted for days till both rooms, two on each side of the entry hallway, were red and white. Only the living room and bedrooms were in this color scheme. There was another room attached, in questionable shape, with a shower. The landlord wouldn't fix it up, so taking a shower in the morning was an adventure, mainly small and cold.

I loved Mr. First for his intellect. He was smart and erudite. He loved discussions, looked for a deeper meaning, was not afraid of hard work, and was good to people in general. He was the introvert; I was the extrovert. We knew each other so well, and there was so little we really knew about life and living in the world. He was ready for this world with huge plans to study international law and become a diplomat. Cool, then I could travel the world with him. Traveling was always on my priority list as an anthropology and history fan.

At first we were so happy there, alone, adults, together in our very first home. We had one car, an old Volvo, and were able to visit our parents and childhood friends elsewhere in the country on the weekends. Just outside of town, we would both take the tram to the university and dance academy and would meet back at home in the late afternoons, where we would cook, study, and read. Our landlords were farmers, kind people, a good distance away with a large yard in between our little home and their house. Behind us was a rose farm, long rows of nursery greenhouses. Frequently, they handed me roses. We always had a fresh bouquet on the table.

It was a sweet time, loving and caring. We loved our little home, tried to be responsible grown-ups, thought we were wiser than anyone, and made our own decisions. The first year, our biggest accomplishment and expense was to buy a boat with our best friends, and we spend every weekend fixing it up, painting and decorating it, and taking it out on the rivers in Holland. We studied for exams, enjoyed each other's company, occasionally taking our old Volvo to our parents to stock up on coffee and groceries.

But we left about a year after moving in for two reasons. First, the distance to the center of Amsterdam, where our lives played out, became a source of irritation and a waste of time on public transportation. Second, our relationship with our landlords soured after we found out they were against the use of medical intervention on religious grounds and left their beautiful 8-year-old granddaughter, who always played in the yard, to die because of lack of medical help. We were appalled, disappointed, and not at all aware of any other religious practice than the ones we had been taught, which was not necessarily on solid grounds either, as both our parents were not church going. I had been in and out of churches and attended some camps—mainly out of curiosity, my ex-roommates in the attic, and a solid belief in God. However, most of my knowledge was firmly self-taught as well as through experiences with others.

Both of my parents had been raised Protestant, and maybe they choose to not join a church. In my childhood town, growing up, there were two distinct sides: Catholic and Protestant.

Two churches, two sides. My sister and I didn't know any better than to have friends in both, and I would visit their Catholic church with them after Saturday night sleepovers. Mama talked about God occasionally but had distanced herself from attending. Maybe she felt guilty; maybe she believed she was attending to Him while attending to her plants or yard. I loved to see her grateful and happy, so that must have been her truth. Dad had never talked about it until she died. I will never forget when I was home to help after she passed; I saw him reading the bible.

He read the Book of Job over and over. He was so lost and sad, so helpless and lonely without her. I realized then what they had, their laughter, their joy, their secrets. How he adored her childish behavior and loving way of always helping others, her innocent approach to adult decisions, her everlasting words that love was the only thing that could save the world. Everything had to be *gezellig*, a word that cannot be translated, but comes down to cozy, sweet, good times, homey. She taught me that money was not important but that love and helping others was all that would save humanity. I saw him grieve and cry after his love passed. (The only other time he cried was when we had to put down our Basset Hound named Lord). I knew then, in the days that he finally needed me, that he was the opposite of who he was when she was alive. She melted him and made him laugh, and he brought her back from irrational decisions, impulsive spending, or around town gossip. Mama was in the clouds; Dad was rock steady and grounded.

Dad and I talked after she passed. We had some nights that we became closer and got to know each other better. We talked about my pain over Mama, our misunderstandings, my dreams and visions, my life with and through the eyes of my friends. He never understood my lifestyle, was old fashioned in regard to work, home, and necessities. His thoughts were opposite—nothing crazy, just be normal, fit in, don't stand out, and be grateful for what you have. I explained to him I wanted to be grateful for what I could have, just not sure what or where that would be. I will never forget the night he told me that he finally understood me, that was a major breakthrough for me.

10

MARIA MORE AND MORE

I fell into a world of show dance, cotton ball-filled bras, sequins, and feathers. I fell into the school of rock-hard discipline.

My new world became daytime college classes, then on to the new jazz academy to dance and teach. The couple that ran the dance school loved having me on board as much as I loved learning from them. It was a huge relief to feel welcome and needed and I was put immediately to work. Bob was a well-known actor, singer, impresario, and producer, who was now in charge of this jazz dance academy and the famous show productions they managed.

His wife Maria, a beautiful woman with the dancer body that we all wanted, was a talented choreographer and production designer. Her stage name was Maria More. As a couple they worked day and night and turned their company, consisting of dancers from all over the country, into a disciplined troupe of young and hungry-for-more followers. I became the real dancer I always wanted to be, performing in real theater show productions, traveling while sewing sequences on our costumes and carrying make up boxes with false lashes.

Early rehearsals for *Top-of-the-Pops* television shows and high-end annual gala shows for Lee Towers, the Dutch

Frank Sinatra, were common. We were seen on the intro of the British weekly music show, our feet sliding on black and white tiled flooring. We danced in the streets at events, and on the beach for fundraisers for the Dutch Heart Association. We would perform at exclusive private dinner parties. I was allowed in their office space above the studio, which was off limits, and invited to be a contributing writer for their new monthly dance magazine. They hardly ever judged me and my bad back. My scoliosis did not bother Maria. I felt she loved me and believed in my talent. Over a period of a few years, I became her right hand, the assistant rehearsal coach, writer, runner, and teacher.

At night I would teach both dance and aerobic classes, when the studio would open to the public, and Bob would pay me for the classes. In 1982, I experienced my first official teaching position under the intense mentorship and guidance of the talented but tough Maria. But she liked what I did and encouraged me. We danced and sang during the day, I would teach classes at night, with music albums of Santana, Donna Summer, Marvin Gaye and Michael Jackson. Motown soul galore. I choreographed and danced to any song I heard and shared it with my classes.

Miek had been, since the days we set foot in the dance academy building, my best friend. We danced, sang, played tennis, and shopped markets together, listened to music and strolled the beaches and nightclubs of Greece on vacation. Miek had joined the jazz academy as well, and late at night, we would still rehearse a famous duet we would sing at upcoming shows. Bob had us rehearse the act repeatedly until we had no voice left, until our bodies were exhausted. It was never good enough, but we were glowing, happy to get yelled at by the boss. By all means, he was the pro, the singer who had popular hit songs, the superstar, the producer. We were part of the biggest show in town, joining their mission to bring high-quality musical work back to the Dutch crowds.

Bob and Maria showed me purpose and passion. Maria was heavily influenced by Bob Fosse and Alvin Ailey, and therefore, so were we. Movement, emotion, hands, the rake and the drip, exaggeration, integration, perfection. Maria taught us how to dance with emotion, sing with flair, sew our own costumes till deep in the night, apply theater makeup, teach, coach, create choreography, and class content. They taught all of us how to become increasingly perfect, how to live disciplined day and night, how to never lose your cool nor miss a beat and how to always be prepared. In line with my academy years, I was prepared. That's why they liked me. Early is on time. Be here now. Be accountable. Create constantly. Don't let anything get in the way of dance, ever. All of us, in the dance troupe, followed blindly, excited to see our dance work on television and to hear the applause of the audience in theaters. Who doesn't like to see their feet on the famous show *Top of the Pops*? I was so alive, living the dream. Never felt more alive than on stage and dancing. I got attention, felt seen and admired, felt respected and important. All the things I needed to shine.

Even so, after a few years our glory as a company started to fade, we were worn out as dancers, wounded, physically and emotionally, glorified and drowned, constantly aware of who would be the next star and who would be replaced. I loved to teach and continued doing so for them. I was good at it; people loved my classes. Yet, my bad back was constantly bothering me. I was super conscious of it and tried to hide and correct my scoliosis during the classes. Nobody seemed to notice or bring it up. I became a master at hiding my handicap. My students were always so grateful, and I loved teaching more and more. Before I knew it, this way of life became effortless, and I was ready to add another challenge—buying a bar and a pool hall.

11

— · —

DRINKING BUSINESS

O ur bar was not just a bar. Not just a business. It was *our bar*, complete with a pool hall, dart lanes, posters on the wall, and melted cheese sandwiches and peanuts to snack on.

This crazy chapter started when Mr. First and I found that small apartment above an obscure, dark establishment called Chez Henk. Henk had a deejay (Pien) on the weekend, and asked me, after we moved into that wacky apartment, if I would like to wait tables and tend the bar. The idea of some extra money looked great, for additional dance workshops, traveling or college books.

We were so inexperienced at first. Mr. First and I rarely ever fought, and although he supported my busy school-dance-bar schedule, little did we know that this business would be our demise. I could barely memorize the orders from customers at the round high-top tables, or the colorful liquor bottles that were stored in the small bar, where Henk's beautiful blond and always perfect-looking wife was working the late-night crowd.

Henk would close after midnight but chose to stay open into the wee morning hours if an already drunk group of customers decided to come in at midnight. Oh, how I hated that so much! I would've just cleaned all the tables and ashtrays, the smoke would've finally risen to the now grayish ceilings, only to welcome a whole loud partying drunk circus all over again to much of the dismay of myself and my beloved DJ Pien—this was a hassle as she would have to start the music again.

Nonetheless, we still managed to have some fun. Pien quickly became one of my besties—a tall, intelligent, stubborn, and strong young woman, with in my eyes the best playlist in the world and hired to play music in this dark establishment on the weekends. She used two long players and had tons of albums available, and without losing a beat, she would make a smooth transition from one song to another. And in my eyes, she was the best deejay that had ever lived, certainly the first one I knew closely. She was on top of her repertoire, knowing lyrics like no one else, going from disco to soul to blues in a heartbeat. I looked up to her and adored her.

We became friends until her death. She died way too young of an infectious muscular disease. Pien and I became even closer after we decided to buy that dark, smelly, and ugly establishment from my boss and landlord Henk. The transaction was a fast one, although I don't remember how we convinced our parents on both sides to hand over our savings accounts that they had so long and carefully worked for.

Somehow it seemed a great idea to become successful business owners while in college. We would convince all our fellow students and friends to drink beer in our establishment, knowing that was something they all did plenty of. So, we made a deal, a big deal. The small bar area had a huge hall beside it, where customers would hang out and play darts and pool. Henk handed over keys and licensing and impromptu moved to Thailand where he could continue a side business selling snakes and exotic animals. There was no fun in running the bar anymore; he was done with it. On top of that, our DJ Pien and Henk's beautiful wife had fallen in love and their relationship was now on display for the world to see. They suntanned in their bikini bodies daily on the rooftop, right in front of my kitchen window.

The boss left his wife and Pien in their apartment next to us, above the bar that now belonged to us. Friends came out to help us remodel the space for the friendly price of French fries and crates full of beer. Walls were painted, a new bar area was built, theater posters were hung on walls, and the beautiful wooden floors were cleaned and scrubbed. We came up with a new name, *de Keu*, which means pool stick. Nothing fancy. Simple is good, we thought. Business cards were designed, and we made deals with a big dude named Bas, who owned and maintained the pool tables. Bas was street smart, rich, interestingly engaged with the local mobsters, and a solid provider of stacks of quarters for the pool tables, besides the stacks of cash bills in his pockets.

We hired a janitor, friends became bartenders, and closed deals with vendors. Daily, we visited the grocery store for orange juice, white bread, and cheese. I remember the day I walked into the city hall, in a dress, an expensive coat and high heels, with an owner's contract, in need of a license to operate a bar and sell alcohol in my name. They needed to sign the deal. Their faces were in disbelief, as I noticed they did not intend to take this 24-year-old on heels very seriously. But ownership happened. I needed to prove we could do it. I needed to be taken seriously.

My boyfriend and I had been together since our high school years, and now, in the prime of our twenties, busy with college classes and dance obligations, we owned and managed that big ten-table pool hall, with six dart lanes, and a fully stocked bar. Beer on tab, beer in bottles, every color of liquor and type of expensive whiskeys…we had in all. We would even tell others our preference was Black Label. Just to look and sound cool, you know. We had staff, deliveries, inventory, and paperwork to keep up with. After midnight, we would clean up then go upstairs to our apartment and count the register money so we could hand our numbers over to our bookkeeper.

We had many friends working as bartenders, and many of our own bartenders as regulars. Art Academy, trade school and university students and our own close friends were frequent visitors. It felt like *Cheers*, the television show, starting with a few regulars at the bar the minute the doors would open. Same thing every night. The doors opened at four in the afternoon, after college hours, and closed at 1 a.m. or later, depending on the population and deep discussions about life at the bar. Most nights we bartenders would drink with the customers after hours as well. I talked, joked, laughed, and loved life with a backdrop of peanuts on the bar and U2, Sting, The Doors, and Pink Floyd as the soundtrack. I enjoyed people, loved to be with people. Even sometimes had to throw them out. But there were evenings our discussions contributed to important issues, solving the problems of the world, and our own small realities. Customers would leave happy after small talk, an intense night, or an evening of pool and tournaments. I spent hours making new music tapes and was genuinely concerned about my bar visitors, their lives, their relationships, their families, and stories.

We learned all sides of running a business at a mile a minute, but never thought of ourselves as busy. We didn't complain the first year—the busier the better. I was great at time management; we were disciplined and organized. We managed people well and trusted our friends to run the business if we needed to step away and take a break. At the end of each week, our bookkeeper would get our paperwork and make sense of our inventory and expenses versus income. I was good at it, but he was better. He knew where to find some ways to stack some money away, avoid some taxes, and establish some savings versus investing back in the business. Although a weird and awkward looking man, even a bit scary to others, he steered us through the maze of government inquiries and made us money.

In that dark, smokey and beer-smelling, big pool hall, we established some lifetime friendships. Never did I realize that it was an accomplishment. Never did I see that others would admire our journey, our courage to open a bar during everyday university hours. For me, looking back now, it was never enough. I did not see it as courage. I was embarrassed, full of guilt, shame, and unable to accomplish what really mattered—to be someone.

I was trying to please my dad and convince myself that college was important, and something needed to be finished at some point. I needed to accomplish something big. All about that diploma, although it became very clear that what I was good at was dealing with people not paperwork.

On the note of pleasing parents, my baby sister had also moved to Amsterdam and had chosen a career in adminis-tration. Or maybe it was chosen for her, as she was most likely advised by others because she had no clue yet herself. At first, she settled in a small apartment, met a wonderful young man, and owned a black cat. We didn't talk much, to me it seemed she despised my popular we-have-it-made life and my egocentric self. On my behalf, I had no clue what to do to really understand her and made no effort to do so. Everything about us was different, our choice in fashion, music, friends, social life, and hobbies. What I did under-stand, listening to the daily updates from my intoxicated mom, was that they didn't speak as much either and that made Mama sad and upset. I believe she wanted to explain, wanted to protect my sister, but couldn't find the words.

In my sister's defense, I could imagine why she was happy to be gone and on her own. She had left the house after graduation, pleased to be away from alcohol, arguments, and misunderstandings. Both parties were hurt and defensive, and I felt pushed to mediate and make peace on both sides. Thus, it was easier for me not to contact my baby sister, since I had no way to avoid Mama's daily dramatic calls.

At some point my sister had permanently abandoned every-thing and was nowhere to be found. After a year and unbeknownst to anybody in the family, she had left the well-known and highly regarded Schoevers Administrative Institution (for valuable secretaries and management support staff) that she had attended and joined a group of rioters in the city. They would occupy empty and uninhabited buildings and turn them into living quarters. Some days it would turn into demonstrations and riots, since the police were frequently called to interfere with the large groups of squatters. Dad, who was her big protector and supporter, was upset as much of his funds were spent on a school with no results nor refunds. For my sister, it was no big deal at all, considering she concealed her raging childhood dismay inside, as she was determined to find her journey *her* way. She was going to do it all, leaving Mama out of it.

"Your sister is in jail," he said when he called me. She has been picked up by the police in a demonstration on the streets.

He asked us to hurry to the police station with clothes and some books she liked to read. The riots had landed her in an overnight jail. We needed to bring stuff over for her so Dad had time to make the two-hour drive to Amsterdam to get her out of jail. Of course, I would have loved to help her. Maybe that would change her ever so well-deserved bad image of me a little. Maybe she and I would become friends or something. Maybe she would like me. But that was not the case since we just hadn't seen each other after all these years in Amsterdam. We didn't become closer, not for many years. That night Dad drove in alone. My sister and Dad stayed close, as always, but I could hear in his voice that he was not amused.

12

PRIVILEGED SOCIALITES

It was definitely not a familiar face, not a regular. A large black man was sipping his beer and quietly observed my every move behind the bar. He wore a dark rain jacket, dark pants, and sneakers. Maybe a tourist? But why was he alone?

Our customers were mostly regulars, every day at the same time, same place. That Cheers vibe I came to love. We had sweet Harley biker Fred and adventurous Jan, musician Peter and artist Marieke, beautiful model Jacque, Thomas Acda, Paul de Munnik, Kees Boot, Cees Geel. Many friends went on to be well known artists, performers and actors. A meeting place for talent and creativity; all born in the bar (I believe I should take credit for their early creative pathways). Many student friends ended up behind our bar, first helping out then taking jobs as bartenders, becoming part of our lives and this adventure. We all knew each other. Large groups of people would come in, but the "in" crowd was solid; we were like family. Clau, Mar, and Willem would always be the ones I could count on, even if we would be absent. I was grateful to have awesome people around me.

But this gentleman had never been in before. As usual, after a while I started a conversation with him from behind the counter. We made some small talk; I remember he said he was a tourist visiting the city. He then asked me to come around the bar counter and started writing something in a book. Surprised and as always curious, I stood beside him when he told me he was a shaman. I knew what that entailed and was not the least uncomfortable. With my ongoing obsession for spiritual things, I *did* know what that meant, but had no clue what he wanted.

He then handed me a book with the title *Texas*, written by James A. Michener, telling me that one day I would live in Texas, in the United States. The book was for me. He was dead serious, killing my first instinct to laugh. I felt an eerie chill crawl through my body. I thanked him with a suspicious but polite, "I don't know, maybe so," but after he insisted, I kept the book with his name on the front page. I read it years later, a nice long story but without much meaning for me. I didn't think much of it. All I knew was that the television series *Dallas* was shot in some state in the U.S. called Texas. Dutch television had finally caught up. Everyone was familiar with J. R. Ewing, Sue Ellen, and the rest of the family. They had oil, cowboys, boots, and horses; something I had no affiliation with whatsoever. America? Nah..thanks. What a crazy guy.

Years went by, beautiful years of friendships and hard work. Our pool hall was doing well with wonderful staff; there was trust and dedication. Everything was possible. We traveled, spent annual Christmas holidays in decadent restaurants in France, and wintertime on ski slopes with friends. Someone always scored a bed and breakfast reservation, and everyone would pitch in to join in for a few days. Highlights were vacations with besties Alex, Phil, Ruud, Leo, the twins, and sweet friend Helene. We drove for days all over Europe. They were vacation galore, those years. We had fun organizing many pool and dart tournaments, engaged in arts and theater with and through our friends, and spent a fortune on our first "real" painting. In America, you buy a car; in Holland, you buy art. It was proudly on display on our large living room wall, and, to support another artist, we purchased two more large paintings over time.

In our eyes, no one would notice that our secondhand furniture wasn't worth a dime, but every visitor would notice the valuables on the wall. We were culturally engaged, eclectic, artsy, modern time investors. And happy with our apartment in the center of the city. Where else would we rather be? The living room walls were painted by us, not by professionals, but who would notice the not-so-fine lines? My windowsills were filled with plants, like a good Dutch citizen. All Dutch have indoor plants in front of the window. Carpet on the floors, everywhere. We were the first to try out a waterbed, but that might have been a must, since any other mattress could not be brought up through the hallways or lifted over the rooftop. There was hardly a foot between the walls and mattress. A spare room served as a closet, and the bathroom had just a small sink and a shower.

Our kitchen was cute, with a deep built-in farmer's sink, black and white tiles, and a granite countertop. I believe it could have been granite, although I would be ashamed to admit, since I use the American way of "must have granite countertop lifestyle" as a hilarious sketch to ridicule young Americans in my public speaking appearances and lectures. Our lifestyles were far from the designer advertised and forced-down-your-throat, must have condos and homes we now see on television and social media. We had never heard of wide-open spaces and granite, let alone marble showers and bathrooms with two sinks. No perfect painted walls or guaranteed electricity. We just had to fix it up. As a "fixer-upper" myself, I must smile when I see the rich and famous go bonkers when they see an old shack they cant imagine remodeling.

A large, blue, built-in cabinet in the kitchen kept our dishes. My mother-in-law had convinced me that you can only eat off real stuff, so to follow up with her ideology in making me perfect, she would buy me beautiful sets of matching dishes, serving bowls, and silverware alike. I had a set of matching silver teaspoons and napkins with our initials, handmade by her. My mom, not wanting to feel left behind, joined right in with matching birthday and Christmas gifts of "grown up" stuff. And I loved it! Now I would be able to dine with the royals, if needed. I realized much later that this education in ingrained etiquette would serve me well, since I still dine with fork and knife, and I have not seen anyone do so in the last twenty years. Needless to say, in the United States, without that etiquette, a burger can be swallowed by hand and one can pick at a salad with a fork.

Plasticware made its entrance around the time I moved to the States. I guess my mom and my boyfriend's mother would throw a fit in heaven if they knew I was now using plastic, though only occasionally. It is not important anymore since I never became a good cook due to the fact that our dinners were increasingly available in the streets of Amsterdam at decent prices. Moreover, my mom hated cooking and would proclaim so daily while preparing dinner; therefore, I was not taught anything kitchen related.

Anyway, why eat at home, unless you have kids? No one in our circle of friends and acquaintances had children. Some loved to cook, though, and I would eat at their homes. Only one of my high school girlfriends, strong and beautiful as she was, had a baby girl when we were still young. The rest of my peeps from high school or study mates would not even think of starting a family. It just never came up in conversation. My friends worked, traveled, and bought expensive clothing or art. We considered ourselves somewhat privileged socialites. By all means, who would eat at home, especially when you are a multitasker, most popular, and known for being constantly on-the-go? I guess by that time, looking back, I was really busy and often looked like a chicken with my head cut off (though still a cute and vibrant chicken). Little did we know as young adults who were living solely for the moment, that all is fleeting, and nothing is permanent.

13

— · —

AN ENDLESS LAWSUIT

W e drowned in a false sense of wealth during our pool-hall ownership years. As no one had ever taught us (I blamed my dad for that) what it would have looked like if we would have saved money and had a sense of investing in the future. No one discussed money, savings accounts, or even the possibility of maybe *not* spending money. And for that reason, not willing to think about the subject of finances, we just lived our best lives in the fast lane. My perception was narrow, as I really had no clue whether other friends were concerned about their income versus expenses. I just remember it was not the topic of the day.

The building in the front, attached to ours, had been owned by our landlord, Henk, and we never had a problem with the new owner, until he started one. He wanted to be able to sell his hotel on the street side with our parcel included and move us out. He explained that we had to close down and had no rights to our part of the building structure. He planned to remodel our bar! Fortunately, we could counter and claim our right to our business and the location it was in, but that was not as easy said as done because he proceeded with a lawsuit that lasted years to come. For us that meant that we couldn't do anything either. We felt stuck and betrayed. The fact was that we wanted to sell at some point but couldn't do that with a pending lawsuit. That became a thought that would occupy our minds constantly, especially for Mr. First.

Even though we had been together for more than a decade by this point, this was extremely hard on our relationship. Mr. First could not understand the dynamics, the paperwork, the pressure not knowing the outcome. He became the victim, and I naturally became the problem solver. Feelings of concern and worry took over, watching him drink more and more, staying late nights at our own bar, giving up leadership. In hindsight, I know that feelings of resentment were stirring, but I did not see it then. We recognize now that we were not smart enough then to recognize it then. We were still innocent, had doubts about what to do or how to move forwards, and were easily manipulable. And I realize that the one thing we certainly didn't do was to reach out for help.

14

GOODBYE TO PINK ROSES

"Your mother has died," I heard a soft voice on the phone. "She passed away today." Dad's voice was different from anything I had ever experienced. I felt cold and dizzy.

The phone call came in April, late at night. I was upstairs in our apartment, and my friend was bartending downstairs. Dad told me Mama had died and asked me to come home immediately. My younger sister and her boyfriend were already on their way. I remember getting behind the bar, telling my friends Mama had died, and that I had to leave for a few days. Mar was there and reacted awesomely: calm and in charge. I handed her the keys and left, with my shaken boyfriend, for a two-hour drive home. How weird is it that we remember every second of these life-changing events, but hardly any of the days that were to follow? I cried softly in the car on the way there but screamed when I walked in the door.

Dad looked so sad, so upset, and broken, it shook me to the bone. I felt cold, hysterical. I had never seen him like that. He told me to get a grip, and so I did. We sat around, waited for my sister and her boyfriend, then sat some more, till late at night.

We just sat there.

Mama had died.

Dad found her in her favorite chair in the living room when he walked in from work. She had been drinking and had gained so much weight. We were not sure what caused her to pass. God knew. I thought about the combination - medication, alcohol, dieting. She struggled to lose weight, and I would listen to her dieting stories over the years. The doctor had already been when we arrived, and they had taken her body to the morgue. Not much was said after Dad shared a few details; no speculations were made. She was just fifty-one years old. I tried to sleep, cried softly, knowing that her words had come true.

As much as she wanted to live, she couldn't do it, didn't know how to proceed, how to get back to a normal life, a healthy life.

I had listened to years of her vocalizing her thoughts, enhanced by alcohol, dramatized, and exaggerated. Mama was alone—despite the many people that were at her house daily—unhappy, misunderstood, yet at times so happy she couldn't find the words. Bipolar? Depressed? Some of these symptoms we didn't address, never gave it a thought. Such diagnoses didn't surface. Maybe Mama had medical files with endless explanations or outcomes. If so, it was never shared with my sister and me. Maybe the family had some insight, but we were not included.

All the while Mama had kept up appearances and ran around helping everyone else. Everyone, but herself, it seemed. She adored and loved us, there was never any doubt about that. My boyfriend had been very close to my mom and had a really hard time with her death. He had always been very close to her and was like my mom, in that they were both emotionally loaded, sensitive, empaths—always understanding and constantly taking on the world and its pain. She loved Mr. First, and he loved her so much. In a way, he was much closer to her than I was. He had endless patience, the words, the sense of humor they shared. We bought her a painting of a famous Dutch painter, Simon Maris, and he had that joke about the painting with Mama every time we stepped foot in the house. He laughed with her, embraced her, and was emotionally engaged with her. He felt my mom at every level, while I was overwhelmed and actually felt at ease with his mother, who was all business.

Sometimes, Mama's loving love felt almost like a restraining collar to me. Years later, during my acting years, I sat on stage in a theater in Dallas, Texas, performing a monologue as Claudia Draper from the movie *Nuts*. It was an emotional home run *and* a performance home run. My talent agent was so proud of me. The monologue was God's message to me. God wanted to tell me something, to stop being angry, to stop blaming and hiding from my pain. I realized in that moment, on stage, even after weeks of rehearsal, that my mother's love was so big, to the moon and the stars and back again. Just like the character Claudia had said, Mama's love was overwhelming, sometimes embarrassing, but in the end the best love ever. God wanted to show me that I have only one mother and our spiritual connection had been so deep. That moment, after so many numb years, I knew I loved her deeply, and some of my initial anger eventually tapered off.

I wished I could have told her at that moment. But my why-did-you-leave-me anger came back raging years later when I prayed for help and felt at an all-time low, scared, broke, and unhappy. I had to turn to friends for financial help, felt mad without family to fall back on, was mad at Mama and God for leaving me. At that time, I had no clue that I was constantly waiting on others to make me happy or fulfill my needs. I had no clue, really, that God had a better place for me, and I had to come to that place of peace myself. On my own. What do they say about that, the teacher is always quiet during the test?

Mama's ceremony was very well attended, family, many friends, locals, and coworkers came to pay their respect. I could see how loved and appreciated she was. We played Pavarotti, The Three Tenors, and "All you need is love" by The Beatles, all at her own request.

"When I am dead," she would say, "make sure you only play these love songs."

I prepared the ceremony speech and was in control, emotionally, besides the little tears that were constant, though most of the time not visible.

I remember planning the cremation, writing invitations, the open casket, her favorite clothes, and makeup for the evening of the viewing. I remember reading the words I had written, looking at the casket, feeling some sense of peace. As often happens, at these moments, I do not recall much else. Shaking everyone's hands, the coffee, and cookies after, the long list of names in the visitor's book, the thank you notes we wrote. The automatic pilot comes on and guides us through these moments. Don't tell me you remember whose faces showed up. I don't believe you. Our response mechanism takes over. Human behavior patterns are alike in those situations.

All that mattered to me was that she was not suffering anymore, from whatever had broken her. I was somewhat glad to know her pain was gone. She was in heaven with her loved ones, having fun, and a drink…happy. I was comfortable with that, although it is not custom to say that out loud. One is expected to grieve and feel lost after the loss of a loved one, especially if it is your mother and at such a young age. Of course, I felt sad but strangely happy for myself as well. I would not have to worry about her anymore. My experience was so self-centered, so egotistical, but clear to me. Our family, including and mostly myself, was relieved of our worries about her. I was free, free of worry and sadness, free of the powerless feeling, the inability to help her. I was done. And relieved for Mama, she could now let go of her trauma and be free. The whole experience was strange and haunted me for years.

We kids didn't leave Dad for days, till he said he was going to be fine. He honestly had no clue where to buy mustard, had never filled the grocery shelves at home, or vacuumed, or dusted. My sister and I took turns over weekends, traveling home to be with him, to look after him. He would never admit he needed help. Nor would I. Two stubborn people together, both unable to communicate with each other.

Although most family and friends advised me to take the time to mourn over the next few months, I decided to go on a study trip to Rome with my art history group, visiting grand cathedrals, monasteries, and churches, including a morning at the Vatican, as we were invited into His Holiness the Pope's quarters. It paid to be an art historian. We had access and were invited to places no other tourists were allowed. The beauty and atmosphere were so divine, so close, so spiritual and intense, I cried. It was a place for healing being so close to God. I could mourn all I wanted in Italy, better off far away than sobbing with the rest, as sharing emotions seemed a constant obstacle for me.

Rome and finding God in Italy had been such a comfort. It gave me temporary solace and a little confidence boost. Mama was in a better place; I was certain she was happy. I saw her looking down at me, from the bar in heaven, telling me all was good. She even laughed and told me I was a big girl and could handle whatever would come at me. I returned home with a holy chip on my shoulder, ready for the next best thing, back to business. I had some peace, though temporary.

15

DARK DAYS & NEW BEGINNINGS

I was easily bored and needed new thrills.

The years after Mama's death were increasingly difficult. I had left the dance studio engagements and the obligations that came with the commitments of being a teacher. I needed something to distract me from my grief. I wanted to forget about Mama and about the pain everyone around me endured.

Dad was so lonely. About two years later, he tried to engage in a relationship with an "auntie," the sweet widow of one of his best friends who had passed away at a young age as well. Dad had known auntie for most of his life. It didn't go well, as they mutually agreed, after a vacation in Thailand. They couldn't just change their habits to fit each other's needs in such a short time. We understood and stood by him, proud of him for trying. I remember Dad being sad and disappointed, maybe even relieved it didn't work out, but also afraid and uncomfortable to be alone. It had just been a few years since Mama had died. I didn't think he would ever get over her sudden death, he had not seen it coming. Mama and Dad had both ignored many health warnings and despite many fad diets that would enter their dining experiences, nothing stuck. Dad did not look healthy either, and I only remember him being so sad.

My sister had a life-altering accident exactly one year after Mama died. It would change her life and bring lasting impacts and fear. It was April again. Dad called and was on his way to Amsterdam. My boyfriend and I met him immediately in the hospital where my sister were taken to intensive care. She had been on her bicycle and was going straight when she was hit by a huge truck turning a corner. She fell off and was dragged along. Her long blonde and beautiful hair had been caught by the truck's wheel and scalped her head.

There is not much I can recall, except extended hospital days and nights for Dad and her boyfriend, as neither would leave her sight. We were in and out, keeping the bar business running and trying to deal with the horror. She was in agonizing pain. It took months before she was able to see some hair growth again. We would visit some, look at her scars, and wonder if her hair would return the same color, the same style. Then slowly, just as my contact with her had been sparse before, it faded. We would not talk about this nightmare again. I had no clue how she would ever be able to emotionally process such a terrifying accident. Not surprisingly, the fear of traffic remained throughout her life. Looking back, I remember not being able to do much to help her. It felt hopeless. Dad took care of business; her boyfriend took care of her. She was so strong, so resilient, so heroic, and she moved on slowly but surely, over time coming back to be out and about again traveling. I remember we agreed at the hospital that it was better Mama didn't have to see her pain.

And during this time, my sister had been angry and sad as well. She was angry at Mama for leaving us and sad because of their missed moments and lost future together. My boyfriend was devastated, depressed, drinking more, constantly emotional, and questioning life in general. In our many years together, nothing had prepared us for this. We were not able or equipped to help and console each other, and we both felt the sorrow of the relationship dissolving into thin air. We were both so worn out and helpless. My response was just to keep walking, ignoring my emotions, and dive into hurtful and distracting adventures. I felt nothing. I was looking for feelings, looking for happiness, sometimes in the wrong corners.

Maybe I was in pursuit of passion and purpose, although these words had little meaning to me at that time. It was a search for sure. Not understanding where to belong, sort of powerless and unable to move forwards, I stopped talking to God, didn't listen to Him either. I felt not equipped or talented enough to belong to the many artists around me nor the erudite and intellectual group of historians that I was surrounded with all these years. Although I loved everything about art and history studies itself, I felt worn out and had less interest in doing the work to become an art or theater historian and passed exams with average grades.

For my internship I ran a few stage productions for a small company and organized art exhibitions for an up-and-coming painter at local establishments. Working behind the scenes in theater production held my attention for about a year, as I filled a fun production assistant position for my university internship. I tried different things, started professional acting classes, worked briefly for a real estate office, and auditioned for a television job as a daytime program announcer. My ambitions led me to try out new things, new ideas, but I was not convinced I could do anything well.

Doubt started to take over, knowing that I was happy when I moved, but ballet or dance as a career choice was very much frowned upon and still seen as a fun hobby on the side by Dad and the other adults in my life. God would probably agree with Dad since my friends seemed to thrive in their studies and careers, and they were not stuck like me, with a pending lawsuit and an increasingly indecisive and unproductive Mr. First at home. If he was not the moneymaker, one needs to have a chance in life to have a career. The word *career* meant less and less to me, as I was more and more engaged in grieving loved ones, and surrounded by the now heavy weight of owning a business while wanting to sell it and having a tough lawsuit holding the solutions to the sale of our business.

Meanwhile I was introduced to the American hype of aerobic dance and the ongoing VHS craze of Jane Fonda and Richard Simmons. Nothing was more appealing to my dance friends and I than to get out of our common everyday leotards in favor of glittery, high-cut, colorful outfits with ankle warmers and sneakers with heels. My best friends and I dove right in. We drove to fitness weekends and step aerobics certification workshops. Fitness centers popped up and teachers were needed, so I started a few aerobics and step classes a week, filled with friends from college and new gym fanatics. A new world opened for me. But, before I could fully enter this new world of fitness, there were more important things to take care of first. Selling our bar was one of them.

Throughout the 8 years of running the business, although it was full of so many fun memories and friends, Mr. First and I slowly forgot about caring, loving, and paying attention to each other. Maybe because so much had happened, with our family, friendships, and studies. The bar was a success but increasingly harder on us, emotionally, and physically.

Maybe because I lost interest in our relationship. Maybe because I didn't receive the therapeutic care and love I really needed. Maybe I felt alone though I had many friends. Maybe because nobody would ask about how I was doing anymore because my answer was the standard, "I am fine, don't worry." Boy cried wolf; nobody heard me cry because I left everyone out.

My coping skills were to leave the house, go out with friends. Loving friends, like Ton, would take me out to eat and to events with Herman, Rens, and beautiful Anitra.

I would be at museums, gallery openings, and fashion shows. Mieke and I would dance long nights. I chose the dark side of the moon, as it was more comfortable to me than the difficult daylight. My girlfriends and I drove all over the country to find cultural and social entertainment and new friends. These were only coping skills I was familiar with—running and dancing.

Little did I care anymore about how much of a dent I would cause in my relationship with Mr. First, in our friendship that had lasted already exactly half of my life by that point. And little did he care where I was anymore. He was in his own world of grief. He was really depressed, as we now recognize it, but wasn't labeled as such then. We had grown up together, enjoyed so many adventurous travels with friends, and explored life and business as partners. We encountered and survived loss and tough times but were not able to help each other anymore nor show each other compassion and care.

Usually, I would depend on his mother for any advice possible, but over the years she had developed a mental illness, and we couldn't count on her anymore. She passed time between her home and a house in France, then made plans to go to

Africa. Her husband passed away a year later, and her health gradually deteriorated.

I ran around, being a busybody, trying to keep myself occupied. But this busyness eventually led to my affair with another man, without any emotional connection, but not cool at all. I just wanted attention, to be held and loved, which seemed very understandable but was no excuse. Although I felt temporarily pretty, it was painful to see how I had hurt him, and how it led to more fissures in our relationship. We talked endlessly, tried to start fresh, but there was nothing fresh between us except the red roses he bought me. What started when we were sixteen was officially over at thirty-two.

Our business, the bar and pool hall, finally sold to our friend Bas. We were so relieved to be free and had good fortune in the bank. We split it all, never fought, never pointed fingers. We had given it our all. With a few words we separated, confused, not really knowing what to do or how to move on.

I only knew that I had interest and feelings for someone else. Someone who paid some serious attention to me.

Just before our final break up we went skiing with our friends. On the slopes and on the rebound, I fell for the words and attention from a man who had come along. He was a friend of a friend. He just made me feel something I could not remember feeling for a long time. I was not used to romantic gestures and affection. Someone interested in me, in making me feel more woman, in settling down.

Both of us recently got out of intense and long-term relationships, we promised during deep conversations that our lives were now going to change forever. It was going to be fun, exciting, rich in money and possessions, rich in friendships and adventures. This adventure was the one we started, and it was just the beginning. This was now, and now would be different.

Everything with Mr. Fancy *was fancy*, from driving fast over prohibited-access highway bridges to running from the police after taking our Mercedes off the parking police truck that was going to haul it off. I was sometimes dead scared and yet simultaneously mesmerized by his zest for adventure and life itself. He had a job in the jewelry business and brought home beautiful Movado watches and bracelets for me. He wanted to become an airline pilot and had started his flight education. After a few months he moved in with me, in my tiny new apartment. We were constantly doing exciting and exhausting (for me) things together like swimming, sailing, and snow skiing. I would watch him when he had an urge to go skydiving, bungee jumping, or hang on a boat to waterski. A riveting, adventurous life, I was drawn in by the thoughts of travel, wilderness, daring, and passion. Without a doubt, every day had to be thrilling to fill our unexplained need for adrenaline, his need to show off, and his need to constantly show me, or anybody for that matter, more.

By now I had introduced him to my classmates, and he was popular, getting along with everyone, even with my dad who had shown an understanding for the difficult past years and my need to move on. Mr. Fancy was charming to everyone, flirtatious with all women, and always with a compliment on hand for everybody who would cross his path. He won my dad over quickly.

My bestie Miek even liked him, and so did my loving supportive friends Will, Piet, Mar, and Clau. All were charmed by my new lucky charm. I was convinced I was the lucky one, running around with such a worldly person. My friend Babs from the dance studio was always at our house and knowing she had just broken up with her boyfriend, I always enjoyed her company and welcomed her every time. She had a beautiful body, large breasts, and her career laid out since she was most likely to take over the ballet studio her mother owned in a small town about 45 minutes from the city.

As a matter of fact, the three of us would go everywhere together, and fun weekend nights were spent with friends, at restaurants, or in bars. Of course, he would drive by her house after our nightly outings, and frequently he would drop me off first. Over a short amount of time, a few months maybe, I started to stay up later and later waiting for him and complained about him being gone so much.

His charm that once entertained me now left me with an ever-growing sense of unease.

According to Mr. Fancy, there was absolutely no need to be miserable or even suspicious. I was just behaving stupidly, needy, and possessive. *Silly me.* I was too vulnerable, no need to be jealous or worried. Somehow, he made me believe our arguments were based on nothing, and I needed to get over whatever it was that made me feel uncomfortable.

"Time to get married," Mr. Fancy said, even though I don't recall discussing it before that moment.

And after that, to continue his flight experience, he suggested we move to the United States of America.

Early Childhood

Mamma and Pappa

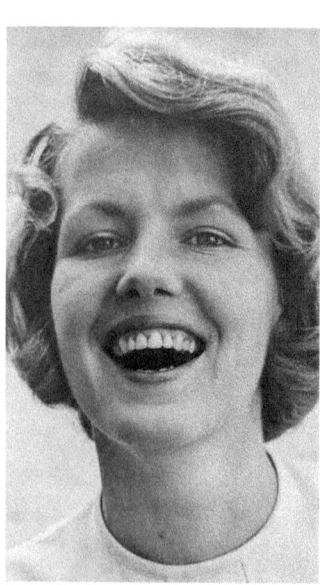

Family

Ballet and

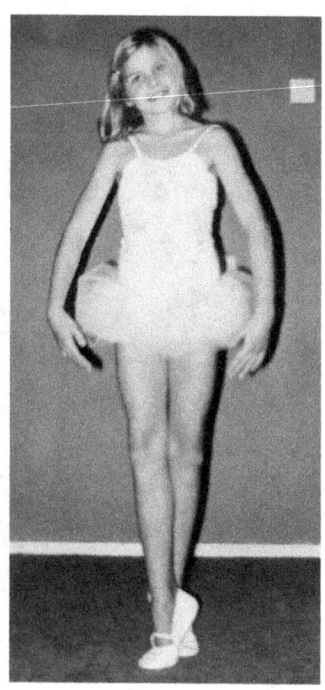

Early Dance

Amsterdam Years

DE KEU

Poolcafe
e. Haan
1ᵉ Helmersstraat 5
Amsterdam
tel. 020-18655

Move and Inspire

16

A NEW YORK MINUTE

After our wedding day, the three of us could not be happier.

We had planned a fun, huge and expensive wedding. I decided on a cream-colored, long, sleeveless dress with a huge cream-colored hat and matching high heels. We married at a beautiful and famous hotel in Amsterdam. Along with our Babs, more than fifty beautifully dressed family and friends welcomed us as we entered on canal boats. The hotel balcony was filled afterwards with champagne, hugs, and well-wishes. We had a small dinner with parents and a few friends the night before, and this night we celebrated on the beach at the perfect establishment for the perfect wedding.

My amazing friends danced the night away to the music of the band with close friend, Thomas, as lead singer. He was well on his way to becoming one of the most talented singers in our country, and is, by now, a well-known songwriter, writer, and actor as well. I was so proud of Thomas. His band was amazing, and I love them for being there. They made it so special. Everyone, including Mr. Fancy, was excited and seemed to have a great time.

Immediately afterwards, we left for our honeymoon and soaked up the sun, sand, and sea in Thailand. We traveled the land, stayed in Bangkok, took a train, bus, and Land Rovers. I don't particularly remember any conversations or connection between us. I totally forgot. I choose to forget. I do remember the bamboo beach shed, soft white sand, and a turquoise ocean. On Koh Samui, you could walk forever, so shallow, and clear was the ocean water. We ate fruit and seafood, sun-burned our bodies all day, showered outside, shopped on the streets, and disco danced at night. He seemed not very happy, and I had no idea why. Still absolutely clueless, I had been taking it all in, celebrating the fact that this was the time that my life was going to take shape.

We were happy according to me.

Back in Amsterdam, after months of studying and observing classes, I had passed the official group, exercise, and personal training exams. I was officially an aerobic fitness instructor and trainer. And, with an effort to pass my internship and last courses at the university, things were looking up. But I had no connection with God at all. It seemed not thought of or talked about anymore, as much as I had prayed during the difficult times in my previous relationship during the loss and pain. Now that things were looking up, I did not talk to my higher power. Mr. Fancy was not supportive of a religious trajectory, and I accepted the "it is what it is" mentality. Anyway, I could now focus and move on, or so I thought. *Dream on, girlfriend.* Even with all the red flags right in front of me, I suspected absolutely nothing.

My brand-new husband went to work early and came home late, then later and even later. Working overtime was his usual MO, and he had to run many errands. I started to feel lonely; we began to argue more. Transferring and deflecting, he took no blame. Of course, according to Mr. Fancy, I was acting like a fool. I was not aware or paying attention to his psychological games, his emotional state of mind, or his confusion.

All I needed was happiness, not more drama. Coming out of a long previous relationship, everything I had been attached to had fallen away. I still had strong ties with my ex-boyfriend's mother, his brother, and my dearest high school friends. But these relationships were draining and emotionally exhausting at that time, full of expectations, frustrations, and opinions.

With not much clarity, feedback, or support and only new relationships to make, never in the world was I going to admit this whole thing might have been a mistake, a rebound relationship. Never in the world was I going to admit we could not work it out. I wanted it so badly, and I had no clear concept of the fact that this was an unhealthy marriage from the start. I was afraid to be alone at this point. I couldn't go back, and I had no alternative plans. I had my final exams left but nothing else. Wonderful, loving friends but nothing but past memories with them at that moment. I needed to go forward and couldn't comprehend and understand at that moment that I had the capacity to do it, even if it was on my own. I had lost all confidence, all self-esteem, and simply did not know what to do. This marriage just had to work.

A few months later, he left for the United States to finish his flight hours which he said was probably at a school in Texas. With the possibility of flying daily in beautiful sunny skies, it was a done deal. Mr. Fancy packed up and left so fast that I don't remember anything about his departure. I was left behind with a few promises that all would work out, and he would contact me about a possible move to the States. I truly believed that he intended to work and live in the United States for an indefinite time.

Alone in Amsterdam, I had a second scare and altercation with an art dealer whom I knew well. He was dating a friend, but he physically attacked me after trying to get me in his bed. Ugh, I was so confused. It had been such a struggle, and now that I finally felt emotionally supported and stronger, this stuff happened again. Our meeting was work related. I had absolutely no idea what to do except say, "NO!" I ran and fell down the stairs, hurting badly. I was furious and disgusted.

Ready to go.

I started making preparations to possibly leave my life behind, too, and I headed to the American Embassy. I filled out endless paperwork, sold goods, gave away personal belongings and stored household items and some memorabilia. My sweet friend, Will, offered her own apartment as a temporary stay, and all my awesome friends organized a huge goodbye party at the bar for me. Girlfriend Babs, our third wheel, was present, all smiles, celebrating with me. I ate and drank, played pool, loved, and laughed. I was so happy to be the one that was going to go on a big adventure. I needed to get away from it all anyway—the past, the business, the dance, and the studies.

My husband and I didn't communicate except for a few thin airmail-blue letters that would take forever to arrive. They were upsetting to me, as if he didn't want me there with him. Through phone calls with his parents, although I didn't have much of a relationship with them, I found out where he was. With preparations made and goodbyes said, I was even more determined to follow him, find him, and support him as his wife. His few answers were vague. He was not entirely sure that my visit would be a good idea. His advice did not make sense to me. We had just gotten married. Little did he know that I would fight, and I *would* find out what was going on.

With my stubborn mind set on going to the United States, I packed a bag.

This man had just married me but was hell bent on leaving. He was just not sure how. He was stuck, feeling sorry for me, but not happy. I tried to understand but truly couldn't. I was going to save him! So, I left my country behind.

My flight was hell. Stuck at the airport, I waited 11 hours before the flight to New York finally took off. On board, I remember feeling insecure and scared but determined and adventurous at the same time. Mixed feelings flooded me: shame, pain, and relief. Trying to escape the past, I left my family and loved ones. I prayed hard suddenly and came back to my faith. Lots of come to Jesus' moments. *God, please show me my path and what is going on.* Dad and my sister had supported me and wished me well. My ex-boyfriend's mother, who was still much in my life, was worried about me as she understood the relationship with her son had come to an end when I got married. My loving friends had confidence in me and sent me off. They all knew me to be strong, although I had made nothing but impulsive decisions at this point and was desperate to find happiness.

In a few months' time, I had left to follow a husband I had not seen for months either. By now, I had started to write daily, and I wrote down all my feelings, emotions, and doubts. I believe it was a healthy way of keeping my sanity. Did I actually know this man well enough? Did I understand him? So desperate and so sad, I wrote about the love I thought I felt, the despair to be ignored by him, and the answers I wanted so desperately. Was I a victim of someone else's ignorance? Was it his insecurity I couldn't see, or was I blind enough to not see, to not hear what was right in front of me?

All these thoughts kept raging through my mind and were written down in a journal while preparing for a journey without a definitive outcome. After the delay and the flight itself, I was exhausted when I finally landed. Hello, America. It was 1994. There I was, without a plan, direction, street map, or even address. With a backpack and a persistent dream, I took a taxicab to a hotel downtown. I just needed to find him, to see him, and our love would spark back up.

Yet, there were no signs of my husband. We had no mobile phones in those days, so I made a 'collect call' to my dad that I was safe. An exciting feeling had overwhelmed me as if I was free and on vacation. New York was exciting, and as much as I wanted to find him, I stayed for days and walked the streets of downtown. Exploring corners, stores, parks, and restaurants, I ate by myself and stayed by myself.

I loved this city. I smelled it and felt it. It was a temporarily glorious feeling, as if nothing could harm me. No explanations to give, no work due, no drama to fix, no smile due. It was almost healing, self-soothing. I had no idea why I felt so empowered. The city gave me a little life and lots of energy. Contrary to my expectations, I was not scared at all. It was a powerful, strange feeling this whole time being so alone but in charge of all decisions. Alone made me feel strong. At that moment, I needed that. Although I was looking forward to marriage and a new life, I didn't feel scared without company. No talking, no questions, no thoughts, no defense, no offense. Just silence in my head. I felt the company of God, and I felt safe in New York. It was the same vibe I had felt in Rome after Mama had passed.

Was I relieved not to have to explain myself to family and friends? Was I relieved to be away from my bar business, that it finally sold and that the endless story with court cases, negotiations, and people involved was behind me? Was I relieved to be away from study, exams, efforts to be taken seriously, and to be part of a constructive society? Was I ready to settle in the United States or just running away from an endless string of emotionally loaded events? I had suffered loss, grief, pain, illness, separation, judgment, and challenges. Maybe I had not processed anything but just wanted to be done with it all. In charge of my own destination.

I bought wine to drink while smoking and indulged in people-watching all day in Central Park. I splurged on expensive clothing and felt new and sexy. Not sure what my next move should be, and without a sign from anyone, I finally walked to Central Station and took an Amtrac to New Orleans. The train stopped in several cities, and I did visit as a tourist, excited to take it all in. Still with only a backpack, I could fit right in. Then I found a hotel in New Orleans and made myself at home. I loved the Amtrak ride, and I had enjoyed some company on the train and seeing so much of this country. I really felt better and was clearly on a mission. Destination Dallas. He was somewhere there. Looking back, it made no sense. *I made no sense*. I didn't look back for a minute, think about anything, nor miss anybody. New environment, new adventure, new challenges. At that moment, the newness was all I needed, and everything felt ok.

17

CLOSER TO THE EWINGS

One of the parting pieces of advice I received at my farewell party in Amsterdam was that there was absolutely nothing else in Texas but oil, J. R.-lookin-cowboys, and Sue Ellen wannabees. *Yikes, right?* Not that they had been in Texas or the United States, but their American-television-inspired wisdom was still well-received.

I took a plane to Dallas, and, after landing, I found a taxi to a hotel downtown. I will never forget that ride. While the landscape seemed wide, endless, and empty, here and there were clusters of business parks, subdivisions and, to me, oversized homes. The city rose before me as a huge, futuristic panorama, cutting edge and state of the art high rise buildings, as in a movie I had never seen. No clue where I was exactly, I settled in, now nervous and beyond exhausted. I continued to the lobby and called the Netherlands to get information on the whereabouts of my not-to-be-found husband. Not much was known or shared with me. He was listed at an airport in North Dallas and supposedly staying in an apartment with others. I called a number for this place and left a message for him with the room number of my hotel downtown. I had arrived. It was now late afternoon.

In this precarious situation, I slowly started to process all this information, and the hard reality started to settle in. After constantly overthinking, overanalyzing, and jotting down every step of our relationship and our marriage, I realized this man had no desire to be found. Hoping he had waited for me at Central Station in New York with a romantic bouquet of flowers and open arms (my romantic dream), this whole scenario started looking more and more ridiculous. I felt nervous but calm, determined but scared and excited all at the same time. Sitting on a bed, I waited for hours for the room phone to ring, hoping that he was, *at least,* going to call me.

The phone never rang.

Late at night, though, I heard a knock at the door. I opened it to find Mr. Fancy. I felt his awkward, almost angry energy, saw the look on his face, and took in the miserable explanation that followed. A cold hug, no real embrace, no kiss, *no desire* in him at all. Although he seemed committed to entering the room, he just kept standing in the doorway.

"You should not have come here," he said.

"It was not meant to be," he continued softly.

He explained how our marriage was probably not going to work out. I should have let him be free and waited for him to sort out what he wanted to do, he continued. My head was spinning so much that I sat on the floor and cried, not understanding what he was talking about.

Not a good marriage? Since when? Not sure about what? Your career? Your future with me? Are you leaving me? What is going on? How long will you be here in the States? Are you going back to Amsterdam?

I didn't get any answers and sobbed uncontrollably at this point.

Mr. Fancy started to cry a little as well. He just felt sorry for me and sat against the hotel door on the floor. There was a huge distance between us, not just physically, but even more so emotionally. This was not the man I had fun with in Amsterdam. This was not the man I had spent time with, in Turkey and Thailand and on a sailboat on the weekends. I had no clue who this man was. He proceeded to tell me he didn't know what to do. Then, he turned around and told me to stay in this hotel, and he left...again.

Totally devastated, still ignorant, disbelieving, now scared and feeling lonely, I felt my life totally falling apart. Whatever excitement I had about the newness of the States was overshadowed by my debilitating loneliness. Like always, someone I loved left me.

He showed up sometime late morning the next day. He was sort of mad and upset that his schedule had to change for me. Over the next two days, he drove me around on his time, explained the tollway and surroundings to me as a professional tourist guide, kept his distance, and avoided questions. I felt dull and took it all in like a puppet, hoping my presence would bring back happy memories and happy times together. Nothing seemed to touch him emotionally. He was cold.

First, we rented a one-bedroom apartment in North Dallas, as a married couple on paper, and he left me there in the afternoon. I paid the rent with my credit card. He didn't explain much, said no to being in love anymore, and said he had to sort things out (whatever that was). He was busy, out of time, and had to run.

On the second day, he came over for a little while and shared that he could not explain anything now as it was all way too complicated for him, and he had to take care of business.

He would have to return to Amsterdam the next day for business. What the fuck? I was in hell and cried myself to sleep. I walked to a supermarket that night, bought wine and crackers, and discovered then and there that, in Texas, nothing is nearby, everybody drives a car, and it's hotter than hell. My emotional torment now also felt like a literal hell.

After a few days, I started to move around. I was confused, numb, and had so many questions but no answers. I didn't hear from him or anyone else. Presumably, nobody knew anything. Somehow, oddly enough, I started to feel a little energy and curiosity. I was lonely but determined to make something work for the moment. It was obvious that there was no turning back for a while, and I had no idea what would happen to my marriage.

The weather was beautiful, something I was grateful for. The sweltering heat was not something I was used to, but I could acclimate. Obviously, I had to purchase a car here. You couldn't do anything without one, so I found a bright red, second-hand Fiat convertible. It was ugly, but it worked. That car gave me instant superpowers as I could move around independently. I had never imagined driving a car without a top, and it was such an amazing, sexy feeling. My first convertible...hot stuff.

There was a gorgeous pool between the apartment buildings, and I thought my apartment was beautiful. Compared to Amsterdam, it had carpeting, a bath and shower, nice small kitchen, working electricity—lights which were super exciting features. I went to the pool and met a new friend, Melanie, and her daughter. She invited me over, and she would show me around town. I really loved my little place, as I had not seen anything else and had nothing to compare it to. I purchased bedding, pillows, and a mattress and put it on the floor. I didn't need much and was happy with my dollar store candles and some pictures on the walls. I found a small couch at a garage sale, a fun experience as well. Garage sales were new to me. Everything was new to me.

The supermarket was so huge. The aisles were so full of so many choices. I would fall asleep from an overload of impressions after spending hours wandering the grocery store. Why was it open 24/7? I found myself endlessly wandering for hours. I took it all in for days at a time—the wide-open spaces, the vibe, the Texas heat.

I tried to find some distraction driving around during these first few days and cried myself to sleep at night. Sometimes, I tried to call home to find out if anyone in his family knew where he could be. No one answered. Did he seriously go back to Amsterdam? Was it indeed for business, and if so, was he coming back to Dallas at all?

A week later, I got a call.

I had purchased a cell phone and left my number, hoping it would be passed on. My dear friend from Amsterdam called, worried, and concerned, asking me how and what I was doing. Not sure how to explain my situation, while also wanting to impress her with a romantic rendezvous kind of story, I told her I made it but was alone for the moment. Trying to find a believable excuse, she told me the obvious truth.

"You know he lives with her, right?" her voice cracked through the phone. "He moved in with your friend, that girl from dance, Bab, who was always at your house? He came back and moved in with her."

My world went black. I could have known. How? I didn't see it, didn't understand it. My husband and our very good friend? *What the actual fuck?*

104

Not sure how long I drowned in this situation—realization, endless self-pity, stupidity, loss of self-esteem, should have/would have/could have—but it certainly felt like a lifetime. It still feels stupid. I had been nothing but blind to not know, to not feel, that there was something wrong all the time during this relationship that had started on a rebound for both of us anyway. It was not healthy, not real, but I believed every lie that he told. I looked beyond all the compliments and attention other women were getting, thinking that I was the special one, the lucky one. I never saw it coming. Wow!

18

---•---

RICE, CURRY, AND MOROCCAN TEAPOTS

There was a way to find out more, and I now felt an intense anger, defeat, and curious urge for more information, more confirmation, regarding my stupidity and blind need for a "grown up" marriage. I pursued the dreams of Wisteria Lane, picture-perfect for the perfect family in the making. I decided to visit with the people that had been around him, to go to his stomping grounds, to visit the flight school and his dorm mates, to get some stories, and try to understand the how and why. The place was not far from my apartment, maybe a 20-minute drive. But before I could drive over and gain the courage to do so, a friend of my asshole of a cheating husband, a pilot from India, called me and picked me up.

He donned a baseball cap, t-shirt, jeans, and black boots. His demeanor was very calm and in charge. He seemed a little dominant, with a strong Indian accent but spoke in a soft yet determined and resolute voice. He was honest and humble. I could feel that immediately, although I did not consider myself a great judge of character at that moment—considering my recent adventures with Mr. Fancy...*UGH*—and reflecting on my past, the friendships I had made all these years. I dared to trust my instincts. Regardless, safe or not, trustworthy or not, I was in a shitty situation and needed people.

I was desperate for help, distraction, and answers. He was a sweet, different soul. He had sympathy for my situation, some understanding, or maybe he had alternate reasons to be nice? I thought about that. Why help some stranger you don't even know? This gentleman had lived as a roommate with Mr. Adventure and had some answers, and he brought these answers to me first and foremost. Not things I wanted to hear, obviously. To my now somewhat dull feeling surprise, my miserable, now *Ex*-husband had indeed not mentioned my upcoming arrival to anyone, had not shown pride and excitement about being married, and had been partying around town as a single dude, making phone calls to Amsterdam but obviously not to me.

At this time, this gentleman's willingness to get me out of my apartment and help me get around in my new environment was greatly appreciated. I needed some distraction, and I got it. Before I thought about what I should really do in my situation, or take time to mourn and cry, I ran out and followed others. In no time, I met a lot of people—mostly sweet, young, adventurous foreigners, who were busy shopping American-style, enjoying the American apartment lifestyle, socializing, celebrating their native traditions together, and flying airplanes at this small airport in North Dallas. I met my incredible friend, Tee, who oversaw the international school and who made sure everyone was taken care of no matter how far they were away from home. She was the matriarch, the VP. She offered me some administrative work at the school and took me under her wing as well. Tee had met Mr. Fancy, knew his kind, knew something was up, didn't like him, and was not impressed. In a manner of speaking, she never left my side again, even though I left her behind many times.

Unlike my previous relationship, Mr. Faithful was upfront with me about his inability to make promises for a future as he would have to return to India soon. It quickly became an interim romance. It kept me entertained, busy, and comfortable in my new environment. Plus, he came with roommates and friends. We were hardly ever alone.

It also kept me from moving on, but since I had no clue what to do with my life or where to live it, I made no moves. Indecisive, angry, scared, and excited at the same time, I tried to live day-to-day to make it through. Some days were filled with sadness, crying over spilled milk and terribly homesick. Other days, I was just being a new person in a new world, without past, history, story, or identity. It felt as if I could be anyone; there was nothing to tell or nothing that tied me to anything or anybody. Not alone, but lonely. The making of a new me was a very slow process.

While others in their mid-thirties were married with children, I regressed back to my twenties with my new friends. My progress towards adulthood was halted during this time, and my mind was void of all grown-up thoughts. I was just thinking about surviving in this new, weird country and thankful for my new friends that guided me through my state of culture-shock and being emotionally distraught. They certainly saved me from running back to my ex-husband and/or killing him and his, excuse me, *bitch* in their cozy little apartment in Amsterdam.

I had no clear picture of future life, career opportunities, or even where to make money in Texas. So, I started to do what I knew best: I applied at several fitness places and restaurants to fill time and get busy. Luckily, my boss at the President's Club, later called Bally's Fitness, was happy with my step classes and the happy clients I brought in. She sent me all over town to several affiliated clubs, and I started making some money as, by the end of the year, I was teaching around 10 hours of classes a week. I added the 24-Hour Fitness Gym and some other big fitness centers and taught 6 am morning classes in these gyms where I showed up in their logo-colored shorts and shirts. While hiding my disabled, scoliosis back and, at the same time, constantly correcting my spine and working out, I know now that that saved my life and my back. I had no clue at that time that the benefits of exercise (in general and in recovery) would become the topic of my now-infamous speaking engagements on posture correction, the healing capacities of exercise, and saving your life by staying in shape while drinking all night.

All these years, I always enjoyed working with people and loved to help them get in shape and feel healthier. It was definitely my happy place. And I was good at it, but that was something I didn't see at that time. Somehow, it was hard for me to embrace a compliment or to understand and accept that I was able to make a difference in people's lives.

As someone with imposter syndrome, it would take me another lifetime to acknowledge and celebrate my own unique capacities. This teaching fitness thing was my happy place. Unfortunately, I did not know enough people in the fitness industry yet to hear about career opportunities, continuing education, or the next big thing. For me, it was a lonely place, and I still felt judged by others. I was not brave enough to call it a career. It felt like others around me were still dismissing the aerobic industry as superficial, a go-teach-your-girlfriends-in-the-garage kind of thing. My past and my dad's opinion had followed me thus far. Back then, teaching aerobics was not even viewed as a career in my circles. My friends were educated with big jobs or huge upcoming career opportunities. I had no clue, no direction. I just loved to move. So, I had some income from my workout classes and working in restaurants, but thoughts and a clear direction for my future? *No way!*

With all this fun in fitness, I became connected with lots of nice people. But, unfortunately, I did not know enough of the "right" people to find out about career opportunities, or continuing education, or the next big thing. So, I had to start to educate myself, going to MANIA fitness pro conventions and new dance and yoga studios on my own. Fitness was booming, and I loved the fact that I could learn and expand my classes. There were so many new forms, programs, and disciplines at every turn. I wanted to be ahead of the curve. Over the years, I added many certifications like Reebok Step, the Slide, calisthenics, body works, boxing, and, of course, the now popular Pilates and yoga to the mix. I loved teaching every single class format.

To top it off, my Saturdays were filled with classes at the Barbizon Modeling and Acting School on Hillcrest. I was teaching poise, posture, and the "model" walk. I had a love/hate relationship with the school, although I believe I stayed for a few years to teach the kids and teens. I had a great time doing so. I had experience with modeling in the past and was confident enough to train others with the sway of Marilyn herself.

How to sit, stand, pose, walk, turn, and put a model face on were all things that came naturally for me. Remember, I came into the world posing and twirling, so teaching these classes felt like second nature to me. Moreover, the curriculum was extensive and included table setting and eti-quette, communication etiquette, how to dress and/or travel for certain occasions, how to pick the colors and wardrobe style that suits your body type and personality, and how to use a scarf in 20 different ways. This is much more useful than it sounds and well-received, by me since scarfs are my signature thing. Nowadays, I believe that high schoolers could use this information. With this in mind, a few years later I organized school-age workshops on my own to teach teenagers the ins-and-outs of etiquette and how to dress for success. Don't be surprised that I am one of the few people that will use a knife and fork on any occasion eating a meal.

A dance company had hired me as well, so I kept pretty busy running around and making Dallas my own. I went to train a few times a week at their studio. Unfortunately, we didn't last as a dance troupe. I loved the choreographer, his style, and his choice of repertoire and music and did my utmost best to keep up with the demands. But this admiration was short-lived after two eye-opening events.

Once, while performing out in North Dallas at an event in the park, I felt insecure, ridiculous, and too old to wear a tutu and pointe shoes. I was not going to deal with bleeding toes and cotton ball bras again.

Second, there was huge talk and planning regarding a performance overseas which fell through for some unknown reason, and it was very frustrating for the dancers. At that point, the company dissolved. I started teaching yoga and musical dance at an arts academy instead. I was once again back in step with my ideal rhythm of teaching and performing.

It was never enough financially, and, while I was one of the best in my field, I didn't get ahead. My parents didn't teach us much about money, and although I had a good grip on finances during my bar business years, it was self-taught and without planning. I seemed to forget all about security and safety nets the minute I landed in the States. Thankfully, my savings supported me for a few years. Many small checks here and there helped, but while I tried so hard, I never got ahead financially.

Beside the early dance adventures, I filled in with hosting and serving tables in the restaurants around the North Dallas Beltline Road area. Click Billiards was my first job as a waitress, serving gigantic pitchers of beer to a large group of pool-playing people who would all get louder as the evening flew by. Even a famous Dallas Cowboys football player would come in with his entourage, and I would bring his order of chardonnay. A fellow waitress had to tell me who he was. I had no clue.

As with many things, it was ALL new to me. Who knew what an Irish tea, a b…job, and sex on the beach would have in common? All foreign to me. On top of that, customers would drown their nice whiskeys and liquors with Coke or Seven-Up. *What a waste!*

After a few months, some of my coworkers and I got sued for overserving a customer who had engaged in a fight afterwards. We didn't recall a thing, and Dan, my manager, handled the situation himself so we didn't have to appear in court. Since I had worked in this industry and had owned a bar myself, I couldn't believe that you could get sued over alcohol. *Would one not take responsibility for himself?* What the heck? Mind blowing to me.

This lawsuit was followed by another minor business drama when I burned my arm after accidentally tipping a burning pot with hot oil over my forearm. Dan was great then, as well, and I was sent to the hospital and taken care of. I only remember the pain I endured for quite a while. My t-shirt had been burned to my skin, and I had to follow up for a few weeks afterwards. Long mornings were spent in the hospital with my arm in a bath to remove the burned skin and let new skin grow back. I do not remember if Mr. Faithful was around. Best just to forget this not-so-memorable event, I guess.

My affair with Mr. Faithful was a roller coaster of nothing-to-nowhere, and I stayed on it, scared to be alone, scared to snap out of it. I had so much fear and anxiety every time he was gone. He left frequently for India to visit family—a continuous cycle of leaving me, coming back, and leaving me again. It was not his fault as family came first for him, I knew that. Other friends, like Tee and Karen with whom I felt very comfortable around, were busy working or building their lives. Karen and husband Joe had children and became increasingly more immersed in family, settling in America, their work, and their Jewish religion. I remember how Karen and I would endlessly stroll the mall, gazing at the beautiful apparel, shoes, and bags at Neiman Marcus and other department stores with her newborn daughter in two everywhere we went. I was always welcome in their home. One of the most amazing things I have taken away from those days is learning so many customs and being introduced to so many beautiful traditions I will never forget. As much as I felt lost and without cause, the friends I made treated me like family.

For the few years to come, I was welcomed at all celebrations and events from Swedish, Israeli, German, and Canadian pool-side birthdays to Thanksgiving and Christmas dinners at Tee's house, who always opened her home to all who would be far away from their own family and cooked for days for 25-plus people.

I knew to turn the power off in my Moroccan friend's home on Friday evenings at sundown, stayed the day of Shabbat for challah, wine, and stories by candle lights, listened to Hebrew prayers, and learned from amazing stories. I could walk in on Yom Kippur days and was invited to traditional weddings, a bris milah, and bar mitzvahs.

With each passing day, I felt less lost and more loved. First, because Tee and Karen were my first friends I made in Texas, and second, because they embraced me like family, never questioning or doubting my love and gratitude for them. I knew they loved me. They gave me a place to feel safe and at home. I am forever grateful for that.

19

MY FOREIGN AFFAIR

M y beloved red Reebok sneakers had holes where the big toe hit, and my shorts with colorful flowers were faded. I have never taught so many classes in my life, and I loved every minute of it.

With each class that I took on, I could feel myself regaining my trust and confidence in myself again. Over time, working at the fitness clubs started to give me strength and some sort of trust in myself again. So much strength came to me as I began to realize how good I was as a fitness instructor. I wasn't just good; I was *darn* good.

Furthermore, I loved people and I loved helping them feel stronger, healthier, sexier. One of my strengths was that I quickly picked up on new fitness trends, started to become aware of the requirements for continuing education credits and rocked some of these courses out.

My communication skills were great. I gained faith in the fact that just as in the past, back home, I was able to make people laugh, feel good about themselves, and laugh at myself. They were being heard, listened to, and understood. I found myself—the empath—back at work being around people. I built friendships, maybe superficial and short-lived, but they made me feel better about myself. Those happy thoughts were fleeting, though, as my confidence was still rocky. I looked back with a huge sense of irony on my past, making fun of myself, but without being able to find a sense of purpose in all that had passed.

Ten months after Mr. Fancy had left me in that Dallas hotel that night, someone gave me a recommendation for a lawyer. It was time for me to become official with a permanent green card. One of my many options was the possibility to gain a green card if I could prove I had been married until that moment. Letters and pictures from my family helped me make a case, and if I was able to hold off signing paperwork till I was ready to file the divorce papers.

Not a single word from my ex, Mr. Fancy.

He just signed off on the paperwork and busied himself with his next endeavor. With finalized documents, a few thousand dollars, and a short trip to the Netherlands later, I had paid for my freedom and started my affair with Texas. I was unsure if I wanted to fully commit but excited to flirt until I figured it out.

Texas smelled different this time around, sexy with a flair of opportunity. I began to like cowboys and bought leather boots and wanted to learn the two-step. Longtime friends from Amsterdam came over to see me, and my sister came to visit with her boyfriend. I felt recharged, loved, smiled, showing everyone around like I owned the place. We played tourists in Fort Worth, saw the Ewing Ranch, listened to country music, and drove to far away lakes and wide-open spaces. If I was not in classes or at work, I was fully wrapped up in my foreign love affair with Texas. Its cologne was different from others. Texas did not reek like rusty bikes in the canal waters. It was fragranced with corn fields and steaming hot grease. From the word on the street at home, I came here with so many misconceptions. Sue Ellen and J. R., football and baseball, horses, and mud. And little did I know it had SO much more to offer? My curiosity was enticed.

Amid my usual nomad-lifestyle of moving and working in lots of different places, I made it a priority to find a new faith community and find a church. I had a strong desire to belong and make up with my God.

The pastor of the new church I had been visiting with one of my aerobics class buddies came to visit me in person at home. It was a courtesy visit, a drop-in to get to know your congregation. He was a welcome guest to my new apartment in North Dallas, and although my place looked pretty and homey, I must have looked like a lost soul to him. The pastor asked me if I was married and continued to tell me not to be involved with a man unless I plan to marry him. And I should be in church on Wednesdays as well as commit to service groups. Fresh out of a marriage that didn't end well, needless to say, I was put off by his message. I didn't plan on marriage *ever again.* Nor involve myself with church groups. Besides, why was this gentleman telling me what to do? Weird, all these rules. I wanted religion but was not ready to do something for God in return. It all made me uncomfortable, so I didn't go back. His message was not my cup of tea.

An old high school friend came to visit on his way to New Zealand where he now worked. I loved having my friends over, to soothe my home sickness, and speak Dutch, of course. I kept telling him that I was in the best place ever and didn't want to show my fears and insecurities. I didn't want to worry him, had no answers for prying questions anyway, and knew he loved me and would worry. An expert at faking it, I put on my happy face to impress him.

About 18 months after landing in Texas, my friend Tee offered me a room in her house. It was perfect in many ways. I would pay some rent and grocery money but could also save toward the new life I wanted to create for myself. Tee always helped me out, as she had a huge heart and an open house for everybody in need of company. Plus, it had become difficult to find enough work in the gyms, so I began working in a Mexican restaurant as well.

Tee was with me the night I took a pregnancy test. My heart dropped as I saw those two positive pink lines. Mr. Faithful (remember him?) was the father. I was a few weeks "late" and feeling miserable but had never anticipated pregnancy. I had even avoided the thought of family life altogether. I didn't want children and really didn't have a desire for children. I was not ready for such responsibilities and could hardly take care of myself. When Mr. Faithful got back from India again, I had to tell him.

I was so afraid, not having a place, not having stability, not having a career to look forward to. I will never forget the look on his face when he returned to Texas. He was upset, afraid, and in no position to be with me or have a life with me and raise a child. Mr. Faithful was determined from the moment I told him that we would have an abortion and never talk about it again. I agreed. Around him I did not stand up for myself and always felt less confident than when on my own. Usually, I felt very intimidated by his steadfast faith in God and his devotion to his goal of being a pilot and to his own family. My faith was not so steady, as I usually felt some form of guilt or shame enough to doubt my relationship with God. It was decided.

He drove me a few days later to a clinic and stayed in the waiting room during the procedure. Afterward, he dropped me off at the house to sleep and left again.

I was alone again.

I had barely recovered and didn't tell anyone but a few friends. I remember telling Tee, who was immediately there for me, making meals and doing our favorite thing…laying down in her big bed, lots of pillows behind us, drinking wine and watching a movie together.

What hurt worse than my physical pain—the ongoing cramps and seemingly unstoppable bleeding—was my heart. I was so ashamed, embarrassed, and confused. I was definitely not well informed and really not aware of the impact and aftermath of abortion. It didn't sit well with religion, again I felt I had let God down by being selfish. I was relieved, but for the wrong reason. Again, putting others' needs above my own, I was happy for him. Mr. Faithful got his way. He no longer had to deal with me. He could focus on his immediate family in India.

Physically I recovered fast, walking around with nagging pain for days didn't bother me. I always had a huge threshold for pain, just didn't want to address it and give it too much attention. Unfortunately, time for recovery and emotional healing or even seeking help and personal support was not on God's agenda. I was on his shortlist and felt it. Shortly after, I got a phone call that shook my life again

20

---·---

AN EERIE CALL

I n your twenties, you feel invincible. You feel like you know everything and that nothing can hurt you. In your thirties, you know that you know way less than you once thought, and your heart has grown accustomed to being broken.

It was November when he fell down the stairs.

My brain has erased a lot of facts and have hardly any recollection of the events after that phone call, but what still holds is that my dad fell down the stairs, suffered terribly, and died.

My sister called asking if I could come home immediately. All I remember is that friends came over to the Dallas house and we sat for hours on the couch. I was single, and Tee had introduced me to a nice gentleman who came over as well.

He was very kind, certainly a gentleman, but I had too much on my mind to date or have fun. Or maybe I knew too little when it comes to knowing the 'what and why' of these dating game encounters in life.

I was in my early thirties and not ready to say goodbye to both parents

I flew out the next day to Amsterdam, knowing it would be for a few weeks, if not months. I traveled immediately to my hometown, the house I grew up in, and found my family there. My sister and my two uncles were present to help us and find answers. Supposedly, Dad had walked up the stairs at night to go to bed, had fallen backwards down the staircase, and hit his head on the corner of the bottom stair, fracturing his skull.

Likely, he might have been dead for three days since no one had heard him leave. No one had been by to visit for days, and the mailbox was filled with days of mail. We didn't get many answers. All I could hope and pray for was that he had been dead right away and not lain there suffering in pain and agony or not knowing what happened with a brain fracture and bleeding out. There was blood all over the small but beautiful rug that had been on the floor below the staircase.

The days lasted forever. My sister and I stayed in our child-hood home and made arrangements. My uncles and aunties were with us daily to help with the cremation, invitations, visitations, and paperwork involved. Mr. First came over, stayed with me for a few days, as he had grown up with me, with my parents. We were best friends during this point in time and not much was said about our past, except that we knew each other so well that we could get through this intense grief and terrible loss together. He was there for me, was there during the ceremony of celebration of Dad's life. After the cremation Dad's ashes were laid to rest next to my mother's, who we loved so much.

My sister and I didn't talk much about our grief and pain, as we were unfortunately always so far away from emotionally supporting each other. Being able to cry, grieve, or find comfort together was not possible. Yet, we were able to manage the business at hand. The days grew into a month, and before I knew it, I had been there for six weeks.

With support from family, she and I sold the house, distributed the furniture, household items, artwork, pictures, and all the other memories we wanted to hold on to. Clothes were donated, bank accounts closed, and paperwork was signed by both of us in the presence of attorneys. I was in a constant fog, happy to have my sister and family around, grateful for their help and love. Although not alone at all, I still felt so lonely, and I am sure my sister felt the same, even though her awesome boyfriend never left her side. She had lost her mom and her real dad. We were both now lonely together.

Ultimately, after all those weeks in our old home, it sold, and I went back to the States. No reason why and no reason why not. I did not own anything in the Netherlands and did not own anything in Texas.

I did not have anything, except for my desire for what was next.

I took on a process of shipping all my childhood belongings, furniture I thought I wanted to hold on to, art and memorabilia, in a huge expensive container to the United States—address to be determined. After arriving, I moved immediately from Tee's house into a small one-bedroom apartment, leaving her without a clear explanation. I was not in the mood, better off to not to talk about the extreme loss I felt. All I wanted was to find a small place for myself, a new apartment, see friends at the poolside, and find a new job. Bring on the distraction.

21

GOD SHOWS UP IN AWKWARD PLACES

The new one-bedroom apartment, although in a beautiful complex, was on the ground floor. My new, hot, convertible Chrysler Le Baron (sexy to me) was parked in the front under covered parking that I probably paid a fortune for. Not the best choice at all since a loud constantly fighting couple were determined to have nightly make-up sex. I had to listen; it couldn't be helped. So much for apartment living. There were no options but earbuds, and I was not ever going to be seen with those hanging from my ears.

My container with boxes of stuff and furniture arrived, and I started creating moments of the past, hanging on to antique furniture built by my ancestors, kitchen gadgets used by my mom, and unpacking the ultimate scarf collection she had always worn. With each piece, I felt a little less alone, a little less lost. Picture albums from both sides of the family held shots from early 1900 in brownish, cream-colored frames. I even remember settling in to watch the funeral of Princess Diana on the floor of my bedroom. I did not get to rest in my new nest soon though as I was off to the country Peru.

A Christian group of mission workers from all over the U.S. had invited me to join them in their work. I knew one of the ladies and thought it might bring me comfort. And embracing God's work would bring us closer, so I didn't hesitate to say yes. We met at the Dallas airport. I didn't know anyone, but I made friends easily. Timing was perfect to become a missionary in Peru. I could grieve, just as I had done after Mama's death in Rome. I could be far away. I could find quiet time and help many others at the same time.

Maybe that was my mission, helping others with my pain. After we landed in Lima, I noticed immediately the beauty of the capital, with its dichotomy of new and old—monumental historic buildings and the McDonald's on the center square. The bus took us through the city alongside the Wall of Shame, which divides the capital's rich neighborhoods from its poor ones.

Our hotel was shabby but safe and close to Villa El Salvador, the large urban residential district on the outskirts of Lima, where we would work. I realized I had traveled much but never encountered the poverty I was about to see. The families we worked with lived in multicolored plywood and metal sheet shacks with dirt floors. Streets were dirty; rats infested every corner. Small, unpaved streets made up the slums we stayed and worked in, visiting large families in small shacks, most without electricity, just a few wells, and no furniture except for maybe a wooden bed and stove.

Without infrastructure, there were few schools or churches, as they were mostly held in small clay structured empty spaces. I had never been exposed to so much poverty, seen so many deteriorated areas, and so many grateful people. Everywhere our small groups went, with a translator in tow, we were given their bread and water, their love, and hugs. I played games, soccer and basketball, with 20 kids at the time, and loved seeing their happy, smiling faces. I truly enjoyed being myself, being human, being around children all day. I gave them my sweaters and the few pieces of plastic jewelry I had brought.

We were there to build churches, pass out bibles, and give our testimonies. I could be a witness for God. God had chosen this time to test my faith, and I didn't have to go far. Right then and there I spoke about my mother's death, my failed relationships, my father's accident, and the way God had provided me with strength and resilience to overcome and move on. I spoke about God supporting me, that my journey was unfolding in front of me, and that everything happened for a reason. I felt God showing me what I could do to help others, that there was meaning in my past. My stories were nothing compared to this suffering, and how in the world could the Peruvian people be so grateful, so grateful for God. All I knew was that I could never contribute more than God's hope and His word.

Mr. Modest came around again soon after and stayed off and on with me. I was 35 at this point, and he had some crazy power over me. I felt codependent when he was around, waiting for his next best advice. I did not feel this way in Peru. I was much more independent and stronger. What was this power? He was surely going to leave forever and move permanently to India. I knew that I had no business hanging on to this friendship, to our relationship. I found a job at a restaurant at night and one at an apartment leasing office during the day. Not sure if I had changed, or if I could find light in my own life, I knew that the missionary trip had made an impact. I prayed for direction and for answers.

For a while I got some. At least, I thought things were looking up. I met a wonderful group of people that introduced me to Shannon, who was always busy and full of energy and life. During the day she ran the offices of an apartment complex. At night she always had people over. She was constantly helping others out, providing care, space, food, and drinks. The most colorful people would show; it was the entertainment I had been looking for. Together we made a great pack. We partied and drank like crazy. I genuinely started to date a little, just dinners or a drink. I gained some confidence and met some interesting characters.

One gentleman I went out with had his entire apartment outfitted with Versace decor, but you couldn't touch anything. That was weird, and it was an even weirder dining experience. Another date owned a tropical island but had a luring ex-wife calling the entire day. These guys were wealthy, as I thought that might be nice, but I didn't get a call back the next day anyway. I didn't fit in with the dating scene, and that didn't surprise me either. The common Texas girl at that time had a boob job, cascading blond hair, and tight sexy outfits. Oh, and jeans. I don't wear jeans.

Shannon and I worked on a fun fashion show downtown together, where I met some awesome people who introduced me to the biz of fashion, stage production, actors, crew, and producers, that would have a great impact on me over the next few years when I dabbled in acting, film, and television production during many fun assignment projects.

One day, while waiting tables, I started to feel a terrible pain in my lower abdomen.

This time I was not aware I was pregnant but started to feel an awful aching during a morning at the restaurant. I kept going, setting up tables, rolling silverware, but after a few hours, I could hardly walk and asked to be released. On my way home, the cramps became excruciating, and I started to bleed profusely.

Once I walked through the door of my apartment, I sat down and screamed and cried so hard, so much. Still unaware of the situation, I stood and looked down at all that blood. I saw a lump with weird clots and a small sac of fluid. I know now that it was a miscarriage, but I did not realize it at that moment. For years that picture haunted me in my dreams. I had to look it up, and after years of reliving that moment in my sleep, I finally understood what it was.

I never told anyone (not even Mr. Faithful), until later years and way after the fact. I was so ashamed and terrified that I had been pregnant twice in a very short time, with a man who was not going to be around anyway. I had no clue about children, was hardly around people with children, and had no family support. I didn't know what I had been thinking, but it was certainly not my intent to raise a child. I was way too scared at that point. I decided to just move apartments again and try to forget about the horrible pain and the uncomfortable days that had followed.

Regarding my restlessness, I moved 8 times in 4 years. My parents' belongings went to storage, came out, went back in. I still lacked direction.

About a year later, my Swedish friend became my room-mate in a house in North Dallas. I had two new fur ba-bies—adopted two dogs—and I loved them. We organized weekend parties, and I started drinking *a lot* more than usual, although the usual was already excessive. Not sure if anyone saw it coming, but I became a professional at drinking and exercising during the day, something that, according to me, went in fact well together. Nice combo…mess up at night, clean up during the day.

My habits were not alarming or devastating, nor did I end up face down every night. It was more of a gradual habitual practice that slipped in over time. When Mr. Faithful left the second time, he left for good. He was faithful to God and his family, not to me. I was barely awake or aware of the truth when I dropped him off at the airport. We hugged, and I got some phone numbers in India, numbers that would not keep us connected. I prayed, wrote letters, moved on physically but was emotionally exhausted. I was so sad, so disconnected, so lonely.

For more than two years after he left, I waited for a sign of faithfulness. But it never came.

22

HOLLYWOOD

Want a great life? Take a different lover every 10 years. Just joking. Meet my second, first real husband, Mr. Famous.

Until 1998, I worked at restaurants around Beltline Road. Then I followed friends to a lounge and restaurant downtown. It was brand new and co-owned by Chuck Norris and Jim Bellushi, and named after their premium cigar line, Lone Wolf. Labeled as an exclusive cigar lounge, it was unique in interior design, beautifully decorated and offered expensive memberships to individuals and corporations, who could then find their name on a private cigar locker.

I became a hostess and floor manager for Chuck's family and was always dressed to the max. I owned "Ally McBeal" designer suits in all different pastel colors, looked bronzed tan all the time and wore stiletto high heels all hours of the day. The lounge had an excellent but expensive bar and restaurant, and Sinatra-style live music on the weekends. I ran up and down the office to lounge stairs all day and night, loved the audience, the vibe, and surrounding uptown hotspots, who we would frequently visit after closing hours. I felt alive. The pain faded in the nighttime party, and I didn't have to face daylight. Easy bandage on deep wounds. It wouldn't last. It was always busy. Then it was over.

The club had suffered from target advertisement, rumors of closure, and fading business. The complex eventually became a Brazilian restaurant. While I kept a hosting job on the site, I was more interested in following up on Chuck Norris's offer to apply for extra roles and crew work on the set of his popular TV show, *Walker, Texas Ranger*. I got my days on the set, as well as many of my friends from acting class.

While I had some fun at different job sites, I was really looking to stay more involved with real estate and I started acting classes. It was a time when I started to come alive! I felt so at home on stage and in the workshops. My teachers were complementary and saw my talent. This newfound confidence led to me signing my first agent, and we started rolling out auditions.

In my acting classes, back home in Amsterdam and in Dallas, I had studied many monologues, and after a performance at the Pocket Sandwich Theater, I was sure I had gotten my passion for stage and performing back. I was great that night, a standing ovation, and kudos from Linda McAlister, my now second and longtime talent agent, who I loved and adored. I was hooked. I started up many productions with friends, took on crew jobs, became a member of the Texas Association for Film & TV Professionals and STAGE, the actor's organization.

STAGE offered workshops and classes, audition information, crew calls, and video and film information. I found an amazing friend in Tara, who worked at STAGE and introduced me to so many opportunities. Tara, Brian, several others, and I became a pack of always working, constantly involved actors and producers, and after working as a production assistant and assistant director (AD) on several film and tv productions, I landed a job on a movie as first AD, a big step up. I needed and had help on set. My friend Brian was hired as unit production manager, and I was hired as assistant director.

This beautiful short film had some real pros on crew, and I remember feeling intimidated as hell but so persistent to learn every part of this business. I would stay up all night reading production manuals and directors' biographies. I started immediately acquiring and buying much needed crew paperwork mailed from Los Angeles.

My AD partner had more experience than I did and ran his behind off for me to keep me going. I will never forget the looks of the cinematographer and sound engineer, when I would yell "Action!", and they were not ready to roll. It was an immense learning experience for both myself and my bestie Brian. We had a great time immersing ourselves and getting to know each other.

The writer-producer-director Marion and I would stay friends for life. The camera assistant ended up staying after the wrap party with me. We had so much in common. We wanted to write our own Hollywood story, and thus a new romance began.

We talked all night that first time. He would call and check on me the next day. I had a huge promising contract with a producer in Fort Worth who had hired me as a unit production manager. I reached out to my friends in the business, people I now knew, that were looking for crew work and excited to have me come on board. This film would be a big check for anyone involved.

I asked Mr. Famous to join the camera crew. My days were spent with this big wig in Fort Worth, and after a few days, Mr. Famous asked me to come over to his house. He had told me he lived temporarily with his mother, and we both swam in the bright pool behind her house. We talked and talked. We knew at that moment that Brad and Jennifer had nothing on us.

As an up-and-coming writer, Mr. Famous promised a bright future, selling scripts like hot cakes. I believed in his dreams, talent, imagination, and lust for writing. Our Fort Worth production adventure had a surprise ending when police and FBI ran in one morning and shut everything down. Supposedly our millionaire executive producer was a scam artist. It was embarrassing as hell, and I truly didn't see it coming. Our first checks bounced, and the actors and crew moved on.

Mr. Famous stayed employed as a camera assistant on the set of *Walker, Texas Ranger*. Somedays I would be an extra or production assistant on set, and we would drive to the studios together. We moved in together in a larger apartment, across from my old place, and started our future together in a sweet dream of fame and fortune. As of this moment, he jokingly said I could be introduced to his friends, and this official introduction occurred during a camping vacation at Big Bend, on the eve of the century, the last week of 1999. That New Year's Eve we thought the world had come to an end, and we were the only soul survivors, hiking and hidden deep in the woods of a beautiful national park.

Mr. Famous and I started our own dream on the dawn of a new century that first morning of 2000. Our homemade fame lasted a few years.

While we were busy working on several productions during those initial years of our relationship, Mr. Famous lost his work on the set of *Walker* when production shut down, and the show eventually wrapped up. However, we wouldn't shy away from the industry as Mr. Famous had his own film entry at the annual Dallas Film Festival.

It was a great time as we had worked on more than ten entries that year. My name was now listed in the Texas Association of Film and Tape Professionals directory and that certainly helped getting recognized. We both depended on freelance film, commercial, and industrial work now. Although we had worked on some great films and shows, nothing was guaranteed. The good thing was that you kept employed on temporary gigs if you were running around with the right crew, and if the department heads knew you and liked to work with you. You could pretty much stay busy. Mr. Famous was a hard worker, a reliable force in the camera department, and knew a lot of people in "the business." I was less involved, working from different angles.

My actor friends called me to help out, get involved on the production side, or had an acting gig for me. I could bring a crew together knowing a lot of people and stay flexible—a good thing to do in the film and TV world. Dallas was a hot spot for commercial and industrial work in the late nineties, and I could hop on as production assistant, assistant director, or unit production manager. I enjoyed the work and fun that came with it, but I was certainly not equipped for the long haul.

My friends, Tara and casting director Deb, kept me busy with movie roles, theater jobs, and assisting with casting or production gigs. We kept our heads above water for a while, moving into a bigger apartment, and having a great time at work and at home. I stayed involved with acting classes, met such talented friends, and enjoyed being part of stage productions and film work. Not huge nor memorable roles but who doesn't love to have an acting role when you can scream in fear or be buried alive in a horror flick?

Tara and I hosted the talent show *Expose* for at least two years—a monthly show where actors would perform a monologue or sketch of the shows they were in at the moment or just to showcase their specific talents. It was a great time of songs, acting, and insight with everyone involved with a production. There were casting and talent agents, including my agent, Linda McAlister, who wouldn't miss a show and supported everyone involved.

Linda kept me committed, and she was big time. She represented Bob Cawley, who had started the talent show and was always sitting at the door, greeting all talent, young and old, that would come to the show. Bob had been a mentor for me since the beginning of my acting days. He was a true supporter and a well of information regarding the Dallas actors' world. I met Bruce Stewart around the same time, a busy working actor and producer who invited Tara and myself to host a local TV show called *Field of Dreams*. We loved doing the show where we invited local actors, artists, and entertainers to speak about their current projects and expositions. I remember those showcases and tv show years vividly. They were full of laughter, excitement, energy, exciting anxiety, great friendships, and connections that lasted a lifetime. Even today I can count on friends from the business. Years later, my talented friend Bill Rhoten would open a theater in Ennis and would invite me to work on shows with him there.

Willy Boroski, an actor and producer, had invited us to Los Angeles where we moved into the Oakwood Apartments on Barham Boulevard. I was with my boyfriend and one more roommate, while another group of actors from Dallas would be around as well, ready to explore glamorous L.A. life. We all followed Will, as he asked and assigned us to produce *Actors World*, a reality-style production following starting actors around in their search for headshots, information, classes, finding auditions and acting jobs. It was such an exciting time!

I was the host of the show, Mr. Famous was on camera, and many others would do their real time work and be filmed by us. I learned so much about the business at that time—where to start, where to get information. We got a talent agent involved and drove all over town to places to follow our auditioning talented actors. L.A. was mine. I felt at home, loved the vibe, thought it was a done deal forever. I loved the Studio City apartment, enjoyed sunbathing around the pool, shopping for groceries at Trader Joe's, and the beautiful environment. Ultimately, our production efforts fell apart, income opportunities fell out, and we were as broke as can be. Mr. Famous and I were not able to stay in L.A. I had told him repeatedly that seeking work here as it was unequivocally the best way to go. He should sell his script here, in the middle of all the action, or get on crew positions. This world was open to opportunity here, yet he didn't see it yet, or was not ready to take the challenge, so we ended up going back to Dallas.

A month later I was back in L.A. for an interview with a producer for a biographical film on the life of Queen Farah Pahlavi, and in no time, I had read all there was on this beautiful lady and the amazing work she had accomplished in her beloved country. Somehow, after numerous emails and an in-person meeting on Riverside Drive with a gentleman who appeared to be the executive producer, I never heard back. That would have been a wonderful challenge, but obviously it was not meant to be. I stayed with my friend Marion who had just moved herself to the big city of opportunities, and we laughed and dreamed over cheap bottles of wine.

Back in Texas, Mr. Fantasy and I did well in the local entertainment industry until it all broke down, literally.

On a job site for Ford Motors, at the State Fair of Texas in 2000, Mr. Famous fell about 22 feet of a climbing wall where he worked as an assistant on the site. I had hired him and some others after I got the job as production manager for the Ford car show entertainment provided on site. We had a huge climbing wall outside around all the new cars that were set up for the show.

Mr. Famous was not buckled up correctly, went up to climb and show the visitors and onlookers how to do it, went to repel down, and proceeded to fall instead. I saw it happen and went immediately into shock. Kids, parents, and other bystanders screamed, gathering close, while we called for help. He was able to take off his shoes while writhing in pain. His bones were stuck out of his feet. The ambulance took us immediately to the nearest hospital, followed by a few hours of surgery and anxious waiting with his newly arrived family.

I remember sitting next to him post-surgery, late in the day. Both his feet were in the air, held up by fixators in chains. He had suffered so many fractures, broken metatarsal bones, and one badly dislocated calcaneus and heel. There were torn ligaments and tendons as well, and all was held together by these scary birdcage-like devices called external fixators, made with bars and connecting clamps. There was more blood than we could imagine since they had not only operated on both feet but had to attach the round fixators to his tibia with pins and screws.

These would cause external wounds as well. It was so painful to watch let alone imagine what he must have been going through. And I will never be able to forget the emotional despair and look of disbelief when he woke up from the narcosis to see both of his legs hanging from those chains. It was utterly surreal. Both of us and his family were in a state of shock. I stayed at the hospital but wouldn't sleep. We decided it would be best if he would be released to his mother's house after discharge, and I became an instant nurse prepared by the hospital with instructions about wound care.

Distraught, upset and exhausted I realized I had to go back to the job site the next day. My superiors needed to know what exactly had happened. Paperwork had to be filled out and submitted. I had to reschedule people and close out with the entertainment climbing wall company. Obviously, no one was going to climb this thing anymore. What a mess. Since my crew knew that Mr. Famous was in the hospital and wouldn't wake up till the next day, they invited me for a wrap party drink. After a day like this, everyone needed one. I think I needed two too many.

While driving that huge company car, a leased vehicle, to his mother's house after that happy hour, I was as dark as a pocket. After about 30 minutes, I stopped at a Target close to her home to pick up a few necessities. As soon as I left the parking lot, I was immediately pulled over by a police officer. I walked a not so straight line and don't remember what was said. Supposedly, I drove without my car lights on and ended up in a jail cell.

My recollection of that night lets me down frequently. Blank, deleted memories, wiped out on purpose. The words *shame* and *guilt* were boldly written over the actual facts of the arrest itself. I do remember standing in a cell screaming about making it to the hospital and exhausted. That's when they asked me if I would like to shut up or spend time in isolation. I calmed down and sat the night out in a cold cell after being handed a jail outfit but no shoes.

The guards watched every move, even my potty efforts. It felt as if they were having a good time ignoring my requests for a blanket or something for my cold feet. Sick fucks. I had yogurt and talked to a few ladies in the tv room. The one call I was allowed I used to call his sweet mother, Bobby. She paid bail and picked me up the next afternoon, sympathizing over my efforts to apologize and willingness to pay her right back. For me it was far from over, but for his family it already was.

Mr. Famous woke up an angry man. He was in such a state of shock, medicated, in so much pain, and extremely upset about what had happened. Was it his fault not being strapped in correctly, not having the harness checked by the guys that owned the climbing wall? My guys ran the show and entertained the climbers, but there were a few company owners who were in the end responsible for setting up the wall, equipment, and maintenance. The company took care of business, in a sense.

Paperwork was filed and Texas Workers' Compensation was activated. I never saw anyone afterwards though. My immediate boss called once and that was it. We were on our own. To this day, I don't recall at all who was responsible for doing what and where, and I never really found answers. I refused to go back to the State Fair of Texas, ever. There are so many blank spots, and only a few slowly come back when I think of this horrific accident. I always believed that this event was the beginning of the hardest time in his life, which would be the beginning of the end for us as well despite many beautiful moments after. We just had no idea at the time how to deal with trauma of this size.

After a few days in the hospital, we stayed with Bobby. She was already so dear to me, beginning with the early days in our relationship. She had raised four kids by herself after her husband had left her in a foreign country to marry someone else. She was strong, beautiful, a Southern Belle, with a warm, enchanting, and inviting charm. She always worked to make her kids happy and was polite and calm with an alluring accent that I loved so much. I adored her creativity, her intellect, her endless cooking, and her deep insight of the history of the deep South. She would help me with anything possible, and since Mr. Famous slept a lot, she would keep me company and keep me going.

On the other hand, I felt we needed to be in our own apartment, and I wanted to prove to Bobby I was ready to handle this nursing job myself. After a few days of help and attention from the family, we decided to bail and head for our own apartment. I remember driving his red truck to North Dallas but now with a wheelchair in the back. We couldn't wait to be in our own little place, but that involved getting in a wheelchair to the first floor of the apartments, being pulled up backwards, or him sitting on his butt pushing himself up one stair at the time.

As might be expected, pushups became a frequent activity, and I remember Mr. Famous being proud of his efforts to do something himself. He was strong the first few months, dealing daily with treating his bloody wounds, extreme pain, and without a convenient way to move around. Our two-bedroom place was cute but tiny. We had decorated with all we had, an office full of books, a living room with couch, chair and tv on the floor. The bedroom had a large bed I had bought years earlier. I turned into an experienced nurse tending to his wounds with a frequent visit to the hospital for aftercare and follow-ups. Getting downstairs from our apartment became a challenge. Nevertheless, Mr. Famous became equipped at doing so, sliding down, and pushing himself upstairs using his arms, while being proud of his triceps. After a few months, Mr. Famous was doing better and started his three-months long journey with phys-ical therapy and emotional recovery. He was finally able to walk although he would never be able to run again. His heel never completely healed, and the pain stayed. We should have followed up, be more thorough with his injuries and ongoing pain, inquire more about rehab possibilities.

I needed to get back to work and signed up for a choreographer job for a show at the Opry in Nashville. I started with organizing auditions and rehearsal space in Dallas, then rehearsed for three weeks and finally moved to Nashville for a week with my dancers and production team. It was a welcome break from the previous months, and a fun time being able to work in this beautiful theater.

After that gig, we both started to encounter a tough time. Both of us had been out of sight and out of touch for a while, and in production circles that means that you don't get called anymore. And due to the pain and discomfort Mr. Famous still experienced, he was worried he would not be able to work on a film crew anymore. It required long days standing, walking, running, and staying focused. He became depressed not knowing what to do next. I tried to help sell one of his ready-to-go scripts and had a producer friend, Pat Guillot, call me on board to pre-produce some scripts he had. With Pat, I made another trip to L.A., followed up by meetings and lunches around Hollywood. He owned a law firm and owned the company Movie Mongrels and invited me to help him whenever possible to acquire and develop scripts. Working with Pat was a great learning experience and was well paid but not enough to keep our heads above water at home. We were both desperate for work, not knowing where to start and how to get our swing back.

In the early morning of September 11, 2001, I was working on the set for a Blockbuster commercial in North Dallas. Production shut down immediately after the first plane hit the tower. I was home in a few minutes following this horrific disaster and then for days on end. I remember this so vividly because it was a great commercial job that got canceled all together. I had had enough, fed up with the constant search for available gigs. I wanted to go back to teaching and acting and would love for Mr. Famous to find something to do. It was time to get up and get going. We had seen more than enough of the inside of hospitals. With his younger brother suffering the loss of a kidney and going through additional years of a waiting process before finally receiving a donor, we had been overwhelmed with worry, relief, and stress while in and out of waiting rooms. I tried to be a donor but was not a match, unfortunately, because I loved my "baby brother."

To my surprise and relief, a friend offered Mr. Famous a job as editor on the popular WB reality show *Cheaters*. I was so excited knowing this was a great opportunity for Mr. Famous—a paycheck, steady income, and a huge boost in confidence as well for my sweet but confused partner who still suffered the mental and emotional aftermath from his traumatic accident. This show seemed alright, but I can't even start to explain how much I would hate it years later.

Our life seemed to be on track. I stayed involved with yoga and acting gigs, and *Cheaters* added on more seasons. To secure a steady income, I found a job at an apartment complex as a leasing agent. Mr. Famous had worked hard to become an editor and field producer and loved the job. He ended up in the hospital again later that year, after a fall with a camera in hand. His broken wrist healed, and he could pick up soon after. I had many questions regarding the credibility of the producer and his willingness to pay on time and to pay well. Over the years, although it should not have been my business, money or lack of it, became a constant sore topic of discussion. I saw how many hours Mr. Famous would work and counted the many nights he was gone from home. I knew what he was worth, what he knew. Both of us were not very skilled in seeing it ourselves.

And although I was thoroughly convinced, I would not have children in my life, I found myself pregnant a year later. We decided it would look better if we tied the knot, and so we got married for 50 dollars at the Dallas Courthouse with only my closest two friends in attendance. After lunch we went home, determined to be responsible parents, nervous and excited to start a family.

My pregnancy was easy and went very well. At almost 41 years of age, I was diagnosed with gestational diabetes, so I had to check my blood sugar levels constantly. Although I was super active, I suffered constantly from sciatic pain. We welcomed our healthy handsome boy after a difficult delivery, but only a few days later we were home. Bobby came over and helped, and with our baby boy between us in our bed, our apartment became home to shower gifts like baby clothes, a changing table, baskets, diaper bags, a bouncer, and a swing. Some hand-me-down items came from one of my sweet sisters-in-law, who had two young children herself. We had no clue what to do, but we just did it.

My leasing job allowed us to move into a larger apartment at the complex where I worked. My manager was awesome. I could take my baby boy to work and be able to run home if needed. Life was so sweet for a while, but with bills and daycare expenses stacking up, we decided to follow a friend's advice and look outside of town. Life in the countryside was more affordable, and our stress would be much less.

We didn't have to look long as we followed my friend to her "neck of the woods." I found employment at an apartment complex in a small town named Kemp and with that came the discount on one of their apartments. It was brand new, had a gorgeous pool, and our three-bedroom apartment was looking out over beautiful grassland and endless pastures. This was the countryside, and I loved it. My son had just turned two years old, and we brought him to a great daycare in a small town nearby. Paychecks on Mr. Famous's side were still a source of dismay and much irritation on my behalf. I wanted us both to feel the need to move up and forwards, but many days I felt as if my husband did not see any urgency regarding our finances. We were barely holding it together, living paycheck-to-paycheck, and for urgent and unforeseen matters, I needed to borrow money from friends. The first year was rough, so far away from my friends in Dallas, so far away from everything that had become familiar. No theaters, no acting or dance classes, no museums, no art galleries, nor my favorite Neiman Marcus available.

There was not much here other than beautiful countryside, endless pastures, a few grocery stores, and a brilliant lake that I discovered after a few months of driving around. After just six months the apartment complex was sold to another company, and I found myself without work as management changed hands. As much as I wanted to be home with my baby, one salary was not enough. I had to find something else and keep going. I found a job at the local library and could do yoga classes on the floor in the community room twice a week. Around the corner I found a new gym that had just opened, and the owner invited me to work with her teaching fitness and yoga classes—an awesome opportunity. I would stay with her for years. We found rental property in the same town that came with a miserable, mean landlady who had no intention of fixing the trailer we moved into. However, I was content with finding something cheap, and it had a huge backyard. So there I was: old class, trailer trash, no cash.

The problem was not that Mr. Famous did not get paid. The problem was that he never got paid *on time*. He never got a raise, and he never felt recognized for all the hours he put in. I started hating the company he worked for, the show, the late hours. I felt alone as he worked late nights and stayed in town a few nights a week. It bothered me so much, as I knew how much potential he had in this specific field of work. I believe we grew apart over time as he stayed more away than home, and as I am to blame for the constant stress about finances, nagging him to change jobs and to try for something bigger and better. I wanted him to be home more and to be involved with us as we had adopted a four-legged family member, my beautiful golden retriever pup, Spartacus.

We would always make ends meet, even for my family travels to the Netherlands or his dad in Wyoming. Holiday weekends were big celebrations with his brother and sisters and their families at his mother's house, who had moved to a beautiful home in Louisiana. I even loved to go myself and would frequently visit her for a day or two with our toddler. Bobby was a source of information for me, as we would drive around while she told me about the history of the Louisiana parish and her family lineage. At the poolside, we shared stories of foreign travels where her employment had taken her for years, my own adventures, and our mutual interest in art and crafts.

There was a moment then that Mr. Famous and I both knew. Or at least I knew. The four of us, including our dog, spend a vacation week at Bobby's house. While I was poolside with my child and our sweet golden retriever, I knew. He was silent the whole week, buried in a book in the sun by the water. Unless it was about the baby's bedtime routine, he didn't speak to me. He was not angry or aware that he was silent. He had just reached the point where he had lost all interest in me whatsoever.

He didn't talk on the long drive back. There was nothing to talk about. I brought our silence up in the car, and he didn't have an answer, didn't care. The realization that he no longer gave a damn was beyond painful, even though he could not articulate it (or even exert the effort to articulate it). It was true. We looked at ways we could connect or communicate, but I could not avoid the gap that was engraved in our relationship at that moment. He went to work and stayed away. Although a sweet father for our son when home, I felt so disconnected to him. I realized it was that same feeling I had experienced many times before. I was not alone, but lonely and abandoned.

So I started more and more yoga and fitness classes around the area and had a great time meeting people and making friends. My classes became more popular, and I would teach everywhere they wanted me. I started yoga classes at the ballet school, at the local fitness center, the local public library, at two different area high schools, at the fire station, at a community center, and at the cheerleader gymnastics building. For years, I would drive two days a week to another town's school district for Zumba, boxing, and yoga classes. I loved those days, knowing I was building and investing in my own business, encouraged by everyone who would visit and enjoy my workouts. This is what I loved, what I always loved, what I was great at, where I needed to be.

With the help of my wonderful friend, Carolyn, who I met during a local talent show production, Mr. Famous and I attempted to make a documentary about Elise Waerenskjold, a Norwegian American writer and early pioneer in Texas. There was so much European history in the rural area we had moved to. I was intrigued by the stories and opportunity to tell it. We had a small grant from the city to support this historical endeavor but couldn't finish it completely. His work hours and equipment failure forced us to abandon the project over time. With two community theaters in adjacent cities, one run by a good theater friend from the Dallas days, I started to audition and got roles in some great shows. Mr. Famous would help at home to watch our son, or I would take him with me to the theater. I was so proud of my work as Lola, in *Damn Yankees*, amongst other great plays. I was never a great voice, but I was a well-trained singer. When asked to play Lola, I knew that I didn't have the voice I had when young. So, I worked hard for *Damn Yankees* and *Nunsense*, the last two musicals I did. My husband would support me but would not come out to see me on stage. I remember he came once, only after pressure from Tara, my sweet, supportive friend.

It was the perfect combination with my part-time hours at the library. With great back up from the library director and in my fun efforts to put the library on the map as the go-to community center, I had started annual art competitions for the local school districts, local artist expositions, photography classes, art instruction workshops, and got involved in fundraisers and civic clubs. I finally loved it here out in the countryside and had settled in, much more than my husband had.

23

HOW DARE YOU DIVORCE HIM

In the early mornings, my husband would take our son to school before driving to the television studio for a long day at work. I would stand in the doorway, blowing kisses. We both tried, but we're miles away from each other, emotionally, physically. We looked at homes for sale. Maybe we could try to buy something, invest in the future. Our son had amazing and loving teachers at his private daycare, and for that reason alone, it would be great to stay in the area. The screaming obnoxious kiddo days were behind us as well. Our child, who did not have terrible twos but furious fours, was now doing great. Nevertheless, we had just passed and survived that difficult stage of super fits, screaming time-out periods, and fights with our preschooler. After a short-lived effort to put our son in a local elementary school, my kiddo had turned an entire classroom into a violent war zone by turning the furniture over, throwing school supplies across the room, and forcing the teacher to call me begging me to pick him up. He didn't like the teacher because she didn't like him, in his words. Two days later he was back in his "old" classroom, ever sweet and well-behaved as always. Nowadays, looking back, I believe my son must have picked up the constant underlying stress and unspoken pain at home. Kids know when the parents are not happy.

My biggest fear was the future. I couldn't see a future together. Fear of both of us being polite but forever unhappy in a comfortable space. Fear of disappointing God and the sweet church members I had met in this small town. Fear of disappointing my dearest mother-in-law, Bobby. Her shunning would hurt the worst. Mr. Famous would not discuss much, besides taking time to fix some things around the new house we had just moved into. It felt like an effort to heal, but I still held that feeling of lonesome abandonment. Our mutual interest had faded as I had left the entertainment industry behind and made a pretty good life here locally, and his interest was still with a show that I now hate. I had lost respect for the show and for my husband. And I knew how I had lost "it."

I once knew a hard worker, a talented writer, a fun and creative soul, who had in my eyes become a bitter man, a victim of trauma, unwilling to lift that veil of darkness and anger. I realized slowly it had been about him, all these years. I had cared, worried, talked, survived, but I had also grown. We did not grow together; I had changed. I was not angry anymore. I had survived years with dollar store budgets of 20 dollars for groceries, saving 10 dollars for a box of wine. Our finances would get worse, not better, and I could not see a way out. I was drinking more and caring less. We had brought up a divorce several times, not really arguing or fighting, but more and more our conversations would end up in circles. He played the victim most of the time which left me to play the hero. Any work on the marriage was initiated by me. Any growth was solo work. I was constantly in a state of self-help and self-improvement, thinking and overthinking. In the late nineties, one of my friends had introduced me to Deepak Chopra, his teachings, and to the power of the positive thinking movement. I read and studied, made vision boards, affirmations, justifying the fact that I had always kept journals and had tons of little books I wrote over the years. I knew where my dreams would lead me but had no clue how to make them a reality with the problems we now had. Most of the time I heard myself asking, *what can we do about our relationship?* His answer would always be, *I don't know.*

We had just been on the phone, and I was in tears in the Walmart parking lot. It felt as if I had already mourned my relationship deeply for the last few years; I had been sad for so long. All of a sudden, I was done, relieved as I felt it. Alone was better than miserable together, even at 48. The easy thing is to know what you don't want. It was impossible to know what I longed for at that moment, but I had to take the initiative, be brave, and move on with a divorce.

I came home and said, "Let's do this." He agreed. We discussed it briefly, had an attorney friend draw up the divorce papers, and went to court three months later. In the meantime, we decided, as friends, to stay together in the house until he could find and afford an apartment. Then we moved him into a new apartment together. We never argued, never disagreed on anything. I told him I might date and move on. I felt the need for happiness and fun. Our son would be with me. We would alternate weekends, and the summer weeks were already decided. He would be a weekend dad with chips, chocolate bars, games, and movies. We would both talk the truth to our son, as time went by smoothly and easily. We decided to both be there for him when it came to school, sports, and other main exciting events. There was never a problem with our now seven-year-old son, except for me feeling guilty and spoiling him rotten for a while, especially because I did move on fast and chose laughter and happiness to enter my life.

My mother-in-law and the rest of his family were not happy and clearly saw me as the perpetrator. I was relieved and happy, and it showed as I left a victimized husband behind. I could not save him anymore. Not amused but determined, I decided to keep on moving and keep my head high, trying to make appearances when needed or when it was good for my son, like birthday parties and social events that had always been my doing and planning anyway. Mr. Famous is unreliable when it comes to keeping a social calendar or following up. Thus, I would show up for a family event that my son needed to attend. It is his side of the family, after all, and my son needs to stay connected.

As uncomfortable as it was at times, it was my full intent to care and love them as family. I was certainly not going to tell my side of the story. You can't make people believe something they refuse to see. To this day, I can still feel the shunning looks they give me. The last time we connected was difficult. I showed up for the graduation of one of the kids. My sister-in-law immediately blocked me on Facebook, and Grandpa's wife made ugly remarks. I smiled because she was just that way, unhappy and negative, even as far back as the first time I met her in Wyoming. She had been ugly and insulting to my husband back then, in her own house.

Although not an immediate family member, Sir Ole, my brother-in-law's father, stepped in as a loving grandpa, loving till this day. I love Ole, and he loves us. He certainly kept me sane that day. With that being said, I had had enough of being interrogated and left for the last time knowing that any other exchange had to go through my ex-husband in favor of our son. I chose to love and to stay in that modus operandi towards the family. I would follow the kids' adventures through social media and brief updates via others.

Years later I met up with my now ex-sister and brother-in-law, and we had a wonderful time, in mutual respect.
They all have loved my son through holidays and birthdays.

24

— : —

A LIBRARY, A BANKER, AND A YOGI

B luebonnets or tulips, stay or move. I was not sure about this lake area and the countryside in Texas. Should I run away again, start over? It would not be the first time that I was looking somewhere else.

Even though I got straight back to work (as I always did), the question about returning to the Netherlands rose briefly.

It could be an easy out for us. Life would surely be better for us in the Netherlands because of a support system, and again it would be a great escape route to start all over without having to explain anything to anyone. Above all else, there would be less of the Walmart nation with flip-flops, leggings, and multi-colored toenails without polish. But I had met so many wonderful people in this area, and I liked them. Besides, I realized I could not take my child out of this country and away from his father. Not even out of the state.

There was no denying it, I had become a Dutch tulip in deep East Texas.

And while I was not sure of a lot of things, I was certain that I could work my way through this. I threw myself into my work at the library and my yoga classes. I became friends with Steph who had opened a nice gym in the area and stayed with her for years as the gym expanded.

One of the most favorite parts of my job was a fundraiser with all the bells and whistles. For years it was held at a beautiful longhorn ranch in town with acres of beautiful pastures, a gorgeous home and pond, manicured gardens, stables, barns, and plenty of seating areas to dwell in. I loved helping out with this annual event, talking to local civic groups, asking for donations, and going to the stores asking for auction items. The owners of the ranch were very involved and had graciously invited library board members and me to follow up afterwards, with beautiful dinners and happy hour drinks. During these dinners and lovely gatherings, I would become close to the man that changed my life forever.

After an evening dinner at the ranch with our sweet hosts, I came home and realized I had not laughed so much in ages. Mr. Fabulous had made me laugh so much and made me feel like a pretty woman full of all those happy emotions and feelings that I had lost.

"He is going through a difficult time and needs you," my dear friend said.

Regardless of how hard she pushed, I was certainly not going out with this older guy, even if it was mentioned by friends. I had more than enough to clean up and figure out. But Mr. Fabulous and I started talking, and the phone calls between us became longer and more frequent. Over the course of just a few months, I fell in love with this funny and very handsome man, and he seemed so happy around me. He was generous with compliments and kind with words. All I realized was that it was so nice to talk to a confident person, an adult. Although he was in the difficult process of a divorce as well—his wife was making it difficult for him, he had lost lots of weight, and he had lost his job—he had it figured out. For me, it was time to be adulting, time to really grow, time to grow old in happiness and laughter

Our relationship was like a whirlwind. We decided to live together, laughed saying at our age you don't waste time or pay for two places. We moved into his home in January 2011, seven months after my divorce. His ex-wife lived next door in their second home and remarried soon after. My ex helped move the last things out of our old home. We divided what we needed to wrap up, and he seemed truly supportive and happy for me. He moved for a year or so to Dallas but returned to our area after finding a place to stay.

Our son was doing well through it all. We talked to him and vowed to always be there for him, explaining things in a mature way. The move was not a problem for this little human, as he seemed to like Mr. Fabulous and the bigger room in this new house. Mr. Fabulous warmed up to him by playing Xbox games and telling him plenty of jokes. It came with more opportunities to fish, play in and around the lake, and have a wonderful school with new friends.

The years at this elementary school were as amazing as his private school was before. I can't say enough about the excellent teachers and teacher-parent communication. Sweet Ms. Fran at the front door, day in and day out, year in and year out, greeted the kids and made them feel at home. Of course, I was determined to make this work for my son. He was and is always my number one, but my new *amour* seemed to understand the challenges that came with a child, a dog, and a cat. He had raised two children of his own and had enjoyed the adult children of his ex-wife around the house. He had also lost his favorite stepson a few years before which had caused tremendous pain and distance in his first marriage.

One thing I knew and had learned the hard way was an unexpected lesson. It all came down to open and honest communication between all parties. The outside world, and family and friends might not understand you or may be lost in plain gossip, but I learned to master communication skills and to explain my thoughts and actions. I learned to communicate better. No one knew what I had been through, but I do want to try to make people see my point of view, even if they don't have to. I had fought for a new life, for mutual respect, for true love, for mutual understanding, and for an interest in the future and the reality of things.

By the way, I never understood why people expect you to grieve their way. Can't we all grieve our own way or even just move on without judgment?

I didn't need anyone to remind me of the age difference between us.

I was fully aware of the 15-year age gap. That is not a problem when you are in your late forties and early '60s, so we committed knowing that there would be challenges to getting older. The three of us knew this was true happiness, and so did the pets. Who can find a partner that loves your son, the spoiled Golden Retriever, and an American short-hair, multicolored cat as much or even more than you do? Mr. Fabulous watched television with my cat on his lap and our fabulous golden retriever followed him more than me. We knew this was it. Happiness, laughter, mutual respect, and care. This just felt right. It was a desire and longing to get old together. Undoubtedly, I was loved, safe, financially supported, and in a much better place. Mr. Fabulous and I gave each other our lives back, in so many ways. Even if the past would follow both of us for quite a while

There were plenty of days that the past actually crawled into the present, especially with his ex-wife still in the house next door, and my ex-husband moving as silent as an elephant through our conversations regarding kiddo weekends and sporting events. I worried about the mental state of his ex, who had remarried but suffered from early stages of dementia. I would pick her up in my car while she walked with a fur coat down the street in the 100-degree heat. She vaguely recognized me, but I would bring her back. Then there were days that we physically helped my ex move furniture or bring him a mower to keep his lawn manicured. He was still trying to climb out of financial distress, so I would give my son gas and snack money to make sure he would eat during the weekends at Dad's.

We started visiting the Port Aransas beach in the summers and I loved the days on the sand with my son. Sometimes my ex-family-in-law would vacation there as well, and my son would be able to play with his nephew and nieces. On a trip back from the beach in 2012, I received a call that Grandma Bobby had passed away, and, unfortunately, I was not able to make it to her funeral. I had tried to let her know how much I adored and respected her and wanted to believe she knew. That same year, my son's Uncle Dario was killed in Afghanistan, devastating news for his wife, their three very young girls, and Ole, his father, the man who had always been a wonderful loving substitute grandpa to my son. My ex and I decided to drive together to the service and funeral in Fort Worth. We made an awkward late appearance at the impressive cathedral where they had married years ago, and where now overwhelming grief weighed heavily in the air and among the hundreds of visitors. We arrived late because his car broke down on the road. While the family waited for us, we had to stumble our way along the pews to find a place to sit behind them. I wanted to pay respect to the family, let them know that I loved them, and loved the little girls.

It was one of the largest military funerals I had attended, and I stayed close to aunts and members of the family that embraced my presence. I think about Dario often, and as much as they traveled abroad for his duties and over 12 years of family gatherings, I got to know him as an amazing husband and father. I learned in a painful way what "giving your life in service" meant and what the importance of military service means in this country. I would certainly start to understand as time progressed and my experience would broaden.

With the encouragement of students and Mr. Fabulous, I was able to open my own studio in town. It had been a long time for me to feel respected for my work and my vision. After all these years of teaching in so many different places, I had dreamed of opening my own studio many times, hoping people would follow me there. Hoping it would be a success, and I could make it my own beautifully decorated space with mirrors, yoga mats, fitness equipment, and a place to sit for coffee afterwards. One of my loyal students encouraged me in a conversation to just do it; have the courage to open my own business. She really knocked some sense into me. It had been a long-time dream but a scary one. It didn't even scare me to open a business. I have been an entrepreneur most of my life and love a challenge. However, the demographics concerned me more. In a rural area, it is a tough deal to take on. At both fitness centers, where I did offer several classes and had built many friendships, we had experienced how much effort it takes to stay in business in a small town. Regardless, after endless conversation and consideration, I dove in. Emotional and excited, my own place would attract people that would have an interest in a fit and healthy lifestyle, that would love new and challenging fitness and wellness disciplines and would look forward to engaging in the social aspect of working out together.

Mr. Fabulous was fabulous in his support and convinced me I could make something happen in our small town. I would be the first yoga studio in the area and hoped that would attract people from all around the lake country area, especially considering all the classes I had established in different places. After going over the initial idea, we searched around and found a great space that needed some work. It was so much fun to fix up. The landlord was a great help, and we were able to merge two spaces together. After a few weeks of painting and decorating, I opened my own Better Body Basics studio, with a full schedule of fitness and yoga classes offered daily. I kept the yoga classes at the gym where I had been for years now and started a few groups in two other places—mainly because I knew the teachers couldn't make it after school to my place, and the Cain Center ladies (out of Athens, TX) wouldn't travel that distance either. The years I stayed with them were so precious. I loved every minute of my studio time and the few travels in between. It is not easy to start a business in a small town, and it took a few months to get the classes filled, but it was an amazing time in my life.

It was a beautiful studio, and I had a large group of ladies through church and advertising and was in top shape, teaching up to 4 hours a day. We all felt so connected, made friends, as many students made new friendships themselves, and some even needed to make that first step to engage in a social life and a fitness routine again. I felt so connected to where I needed to be and realized my time had come. God wanted me here. This was my purpose, my dreams, my vision becoming reality. To teach, to entertain, to listen, to share.

The studio became a great place of gathering for so many more reasons than just wellness alone. After about a year another space in the building became available, and I opened, after another fun renovation, a wellness center with three massage therapists, a facial care specialist and wonderful products for sale. I would organize monthly speaker events with guests discussing healthy topics from nutrition to supplements to the benefits of massage and skin care.

In the summers, I would go to my SCW MANIA fitness pro convention and return with new certifications and new ideas. The Monday after, everyone came in semi-scared and excited, knowing I was so stoked with new ideas that would mean we would have to work our butts off for weeks on new fitness and yoga disciplines. At some point, we all did strength training, yoga, Tai Chi, boxing, and Zumba. I say "we" because I couldn't have done it without all the support from clients. It was such an amazing and fun time. To this day, I dearly miss some of the ladies and loved them as they gave back so much. I felt loved and appreciated but did not follow up with some of the friendships after the studio closed and moved into my home studio. And even afterwards, life just got so busy. I regret not taking or making the time to follow up.

Thankful for all the changes in my life at this point, I started to feel a great sense of fulfillment. I was so happy at home with Mr. Fabulous, so proud of my son and his accomplishments in school, and the friendships he made. You could find the kids all together on the lake in their spare time, with mothers Ruth or Angela watching the gang. I had the utmost respect for these moms, as dedicated and present they were to their children's upbringing. I believe I did well raising my son, but I was never a creative mother. I didn't bake, paint, create, craft, build furniture tents, or go out to fun places in the big city. My son went to others' homes to play, and he was always welcome. What I did, as per usual as a "coaching role" mom, was discuss life lessons on the way to school, starting the mornings with reciting, *Today is the day* creed, followed by *Make it a great day*. I taught my son that he is always in charge and has a choice to make it work or be in control. We practiced manifestations for a

159

miraculous day to arise. When in Florida on vacation, we went to Mel Fisher's Museum in Key West, and I bought him the necklace to go with our creed. That's the kind of mother thing I did—constant positive encouragement and long adult conversations. I know it worked.

Mr. Fabulous stepped right in his stepdad role but made it clear he was done with a daily dose of loud kids over the floor. He had raised and helped his kids for years, and thus made it clear we would be everywhere but home at the hour he wanted to relax. I laughed and understood. A relationship is give and take, so it was the silent rule that my son's play dates would be elsewhere. I was a busy working mother, so the school bus would drop him off at the yoga studio where he would do homework or be picked up. On the other hand, we never missed a special event at school, never missed a band performance, soccer, basketball, football, or tennis game and were there for every step of homework.

I also experienced what it is to live with a Vietnam veteran who suffers from PTSD and keeps me frequently up at night. I listened, tried to understand, to gain knowledge about something I can never truly comprehend. As civilians, we never will. We don't understand the respect, the camaraderie, the responsibility, the commitment, the brotherhood in peril and loss, nor the sites that have been seen. We sympathized, but we were not there. Mr. Fabulous goes through memories almost daily, as in trauma. It never leaves. In my work, a lot of veterans came through as well, so I learned and accepted it more and more. It is often tough for veterans to step back into the civilian world, a less disciplined environment where one finds less signs of respect, less structure. and nowadays even less commitment to perform well or contribute something valuable. It is tough to adjust to small talk when you have seen it all in war. Lots of mental and emotional work for a girl that's coming from a country where possession, carry, and use of firearms and other weapons are prohibited. Along the way, I had changed my ways of thinking as I moved through times and places in the States. I can stretch my imagination and practice empathy and compassion as well as stay engaged. In Texas, we can own a gun, and heck, it's a big state.

As I had always said, I would never be like my mom. Yet, the older I get, the more I find myself to be and act just like her. It is funny to see yourself as a mother, at times defensive, willing to strut to school to tell the teacher the truth, struggling to hold your emotions during a winning game or concert, or to hold in those comments and squeeze your kid to death after. My mom did hugs, everyone got one, even my school buddies who would come over after school. She called everyone a sweetheart or darling, like it or not. I do the same. Everyone is a "honey," and I give good hugs. Whether they like it or not.

Understanding more and more this to be such a pivotal point, I felt so blessed, counted every minute, and said thanks to God for showing me where I needed to be. My purpose was to help people, in so many ways, and for so long I had not been able to see it. I remembered how the pastor of my beautiful church that I attended when we just moved to the countryside had a profound answer for me during a session at his home. I would come over to assist with his physical pain—he suffered from ALS and would unfortunately lose his life to that terrible disease. I hoped to be able to help ease his pain by working with him on small remedial movements with him to see if his muscular system would answer. He was in so much pain but tried so hard every time. I loved him as my pastor. He had been the one that baptized my son. In a long conversation, he pointed out my purpose, that I was blind to it, that it was in front of my nose.

"Why do you underestimate your own work so much? You are so lost sometimes and trying so hard," he asked. *"You do not see how much you contribute to the health and happiness of others. You do not value what you do. You do not charge enough, selling yourself cheap."*

I was so perplexed. He was right, I had always underestimated my work, not feeling enough. As I had come from a past where no one would take dance or fitness seriously, how could I? Another thing he told me was to *see how loved and appreciated I was* and to embrace it instead of displaying a false sense of modesty. Immediately after this conversation, I felt and accepted my purpose and started my true transformation as God wanted me to live out and share with others.

During the years that followed, we moved closer to the school district, and I moved my studio to my home studio, a space in the detached garage that we had converted. Our new house took some renovation. It was a gorgeous but older home with a beautiful curb appeal, so statuesque with its white pillars in the front. A dream for us both to move into a space we could fix up together and make into our own nest. How could I be so lucky meeting this wonderful, caretaking man who loved making me laugh, who loved fixing up a home with me? We worked on the house for months, did a lot on our own, as we both loved to fix it up and do it ourselves. How in the world did I end up in Gun Barrel City, Texas? Such a sexy choice after a taste of Amsterdam, New York, Dallas, Los Angeles, and again Dallas. I am settling in the sticks, sixty miles southeast from my favorite Neiman Marcus at Northpark, but settling in quite well. Happiness comes in places you least expect.

Now seven years ago I accepted a position as yoga instructor and wellness counselor at a rehabilitation facility that opened about 30 minutes away from home. Wow, an addiction rehab. How fitting for me, an alcoholic, especially being from the gene pool I swam around in. As I have a firm grip, nowadays, on drinking, I go to work at a place where I can share my little girl/daddy issues and losses to losing a grip on love and crawling back up to find joy. It came at a perfect time combined with my own studio groups I could expand, such an exciting opportunity to work with patients in recovery. To top it off, as if everything fell in place, I was invited to present my first Tai Chi-influenced wellness program with SCW, the largest fitness education company in the U.S., who has offered over a time frame of 30 years a large variety of fitness and wellness conventions and education to fitness professionals and enthusiasts. It was so exciting and an honor to share my ideas with so many people all over. I love to travel. Such an awesome challenge!

I also needed to keep working as I didn't receive child support and had always taken pride in taking care of my son's needs myself. I was adamant to provide for him and get him to college. I was so proud to be able to spoil him at times, especially because I went through the same shame and guilt trip many parents do after divorce.

I met some amazing mentors that would influence me greatly and Sara Kooperman, CEO of SCW Fitness Education and WATERinMOTION, invited and encouraged me to write my own programs as well. I was thankful and excited for such a huge honor to present at this largest fitness education platform. For the next five years, I would travel the country to several conventions, sometimes with Mr. Fabulous because in the beginning it was lonely not knowing anyone well. And of course, so we could enjoy sightseeing and traveling together while I presented my programs during the day. It was a rewarding and amazing experience to connect all over the country with people in the business, especially because I was on my own in our little town. There were not many yogis to share business information with.

I seldom had the opportunity to connect with others, other than the classes or workshops I took in Dallas, so these conventions would fuel me and vice versa. I shared all I knew about the benefits of movement; in all I had seen and experienced. Over the years, I wrote and taught more than 15 different programs, some made available on video. I learned from the best in the business, big name creators and leaders, who were all such an inspiration to me. If copying is the highest form of flattery,

Then I gave my own *Elian spin* to the materials. Lisa and Super Betty always kept me company when I felt lost, and I was so grateful for my long weekends with talented new friends Tricia, Jane, Christine, Yury, Connie, Melissa and Billie. We laughed, learned, and dined together. I kept educating myself, consistently adding certifications to my resume that would not just benefit my students, but my patients at the rehab facility as well.

Speaking in public all over the country gave me the courage to keep speaking, and it gave me the confidence that I was on the right path. God shows up when you ask direction, and you tell Him what you dream of and work for. I asked, constantly in doubt, thinking, and overthinking. Hard work is necessary to make Him proud, and I worked my behind off. I showed up in all directions. I realized it was not so much what you do or what you know, but why and how you do it. Not the yoga pose itself, but the way I taught it. *Everyone is a yoga instructor now,* I laughed while scrolling social media. But they are not ME. The imposter syndrome that I had suffered faded. My purpose became sharing, telling stories, and delivering it all with humor, energy, and an increasing sense of purpose and urgency. This is where I belong.

25

---·---

ADDICTION & PREDICTION

How crazy was my journey? How in the world could a gentleman in a bar in Amsterdam make a prediction about the twenty-something-years-old girl behind the bar? How did he know I would go to Texas, trying to change the world one mind-body-spirit at the time? Thinking about what I know now, I believe God wanted to tell me something, but had a few curveballs on the way, to make me see, to make me a true believer and servant.

The Treehouse Rehab (now Vertava Health) facility in Scurry, Texas, became a full-time position. I knew where I needed to be and what my gifts were. I was on a mission, adding more and more to the program to help clients and veterans in recovery from substance abuse. It was very familiar terrain for me with an alcohol-loaded past coming from an alcoholic family. Besides my boss Vinnie, who I loved from day one, and the amazing staff he had gathered, I knew God had placed me here. Unlike the clinic my mother went to when I was young, this would have been such a loving and caring environment for her. I imagined her being here, surrounded by caring and compassionate people with the knowledge and experience she needed at the time. I don't remember what it was like in those days, but I was convinced the opinions and acceptance of asking for help and going to a rehab facility had changed profoundly.

In my work as a counselor, I heard many horrific stories of trauma, grief, abuse or pain, and unbelievable stories of the ugliness of mankind. It felt so good to bring understanding, movement, healing, and joy, and to share the little wisdom I had gained over the years working on myself. The atmosphere at the rehab center was one of a large family, with Vinnie as a leader who would help and encourage us all to become unstoppable in our effort to reach beyond our imagination, and to help each other become the best we could be as a recovery facility. As coworkers we had fun, we rode horses, ziplined, ate beautifully prepared meals, and played outside of work together. I studied trauma informed yoga programs, gained more knowledge on pain management and opioid abuse, and excelled in a somatic approach to healing. We had the freedom to contribute and develop any creative, clinical, and counseling programs for the curriculum so we could bring excellence in our efforts to help patients on their journey to recovery.

Two years ago I became a life-coach because I was naturally already serving as one. Helping others through counseling came naturally to me, and my clients trusted me and felt comfortable with me, so I wanted the title to back up my work, besides wellness coach. I did not want to be a therapist, but through life coaching, I could help people move forwards to become unstuck. Secretly, between you and me, this came from the constant desire to prove myself. I constantly needed to earn more certifications. This imposter syndrome came from my abandonment trauma as a young person. In my youth, I never recognized this while dancing in Amsterdam or running a bar or chasing happiness across the United States. I guess doubt sets in over time.

Point was, I think that I felt more empowered at this point in my life than any in the previous fifteen years. Living in the Texas countryside, I work and live in a place I could have never imagined, helping others towards a healthier lifestyle and in such a positive way. I recognized the struggles. I shared, digging deep from my own experiences. I was not afraid to take it all in and became a serial certification collector during it all, to be better equipped to help, to become more specialized and knowledgeable. If I was ever on the revenge trail, this was my time to shine. My "coach approach" was distinct, different, straightforward, and with great outcome and great results. I like benefits, pay off, rewards for working your tail off, and rewards come with happy clients and patients. I am specialized in self-awareness, self-management, social awareness, and relationships. As a coach and leader, above all, I deal in energy and hand out hugs. I adapted, achieved, and can influence and heal others. As if I could finally see my why—why I was doing what I was doing all along after so long without a cause, without realizing I was great at what I do, and worthy of doing it.

Does everything fall in place? Was the journey worth it? Would I have been here if I would have known all the answers? Maybe I was told but was not ready to listen?

Altogether, the fortunate and unfortunate fell in place. My theater background makes me happy and at ease on stage and television, my dance background keeps others and myself in shape and healthy. My family is far but near, and I have an amazing group of friends and a church family that loves and supports me, despite my shortcomings, funny faces, and childish behavior. They support my vision and my mission, and with a smile, I say they are used to me. I can relax now, with a proud heart looking at my son who is doing well and learning to enjoy life. This story was for you, in the hopes you get to know and love me for who I am. And looking at the man I love, who makes me laugh so much, enjoying the little things of life together. I am OK; you are Ok. Thank you, Mama, for everything you taught me about love. Love wins, and I love big, and have a lot of love to give. Thanks be to God and the ones that stuck with me because the transformation has been so rewarding, and in the end, I would not change a thing. *I wish I would have known, but I'm glad I didn't.*

26

CURTAIN CALL

I WISH I WOULD HAVE KNOWN, BUT I AM GLAD I DIDN'T

*W*e *all know this wisdom stuff, but it means nothing until we apply it.*

This chapter is mine, my wrap party, me talking to myself. The previous was my story. This is my solution. This chapter serves as truth, as a reflection on my life, and my intent and hope is that you will recognize, as I did, that as I got older, my life and happenings became as clear as can be.

The more patients and clients I served these past fifteen years, the more one pivotal lesson made itself known to me. The more I studied, the more knowledge I gained, the more it became clear to me that so many events in my life were a reaction rather than an action.

That's why I like to use the above statement for my life. I wish I would have known what I know now, but I am grateful that I did not realize what I do now, as my path became exactly what God had intended.

Would you like to know your truth?

Could you find the courage to look at your own past and reflect in an honest and humble way?

Can you handle the truth?

If so, life becomes easy, you will find peace…ask yourself these questions:

What does life expect of me instead of just being in it? Do you know your WHY?

You read my story, my memoir, my reflections. Without names, without intentions to hurt or leave anyone uncomfortable, without the means of dragging anyone in. Just my memories, as much as I can recall them.

You will find out where and why you made the mistakes, the wrong turns, and the wrong choices. You will clearly see why I missed chances and denied making changes. Many lost opportunities and many mistakes that brought me here today, the happiest place on earth for me. ***Thanks be to my God, for showing the chaos and mess so I could come to the light and become enlightened.***

Let's talk about expectation versus transformation.

Often, we don't realize we live in a world of expectations. We do what our parents expect of us, then conform in our twenties into the perfect students, contribute to society in the workforce, or start a family. Followed by a "perfect picture" route of perfect marriage, children, and the three-bedroom, two-bath house down Wisteria Lane. The front and back yards need to be manicured. In the wide open spaces, we need guest rooms for friends and in-laws, the perfect nursery, many bedrooms for our little ones who all need their own space. We can't live without the granite countertop and perfect manicured nails. This is the world we created at the end of the last decades, on television and social media.

But what if nobody taught us how to keep up with all that and work three jobs per person to pay off the loans that bought it? We become exhausted, puppets to expectations, a shadow of our former innocent and joyful self. That's when self-doubt, negative thinking and resentment settles in, with symptoms of anxiety and depression, symptoms of disease, unease, that are manifesting and fostering in the mind and body.

Transformation comes when we go back to our inner voice and take the time to reflect, pray, and listen to our souls. You are an actor on your own stage. You just have to write the script or playbook and define your dreams, your wishes. It might cause pain and hurt to get there, sometimes even abandonment of people and places you thought you loved or belonged to. It takes courage to leave your comfort zone and pursue your dreams, but it is the only way to self-love, inspiration, creativity, and your purpose, given to your unique self by your higher power. I went all the way the last 20 years, in search of self, my purpose, my missions and visions, on a deep transformation path. My peace comes from a deep, joyful place inside and is unbeknownst any circumstances, always at peace. It is undisturbed. I go through the emotional rollercoaster just like anyone else, in times of pain, suffering, sorrow, or loss, but I am at peace knowing the outcome is in my God's hands. My happiness does not depend on people, places, circumstances, and events anymore. I became a warrior instead of a worrier.

Life does not get any easier, you just get better at it.

27

VETO YOUR GUILT AND SHAME

These two emotions will follow you endlessly. You might be like me—where for the longest time I didn't understand that emotions don't serve me. Nowadays, I explain to my patients that guilt is the emotion you feel regarding something you did to others—a selfish act of stupidity, a revenge, an anger driven event, a hurtful accumulation of unhealthy decisions. I had many of these days where I was sorry for my actions, not wanting to think about the consequences, or mad enough to go through with it anyway. Instead of a good conversation with my higher power of an angel friend, I had to be in control and play victim (to my circumstances) instead of victor. It would have been easier to accept that Jesus had died for my sins, that I was forgiven, and that I could move on. Difficult? Yes, always, but a shorter way to happiness indeed.

Shame comes in the form of self (towards the inner self), as in not being proud and ashamed of what has been said or done. Shame for me had to do with my relationship with my God, trying to live up to the perfect expectations, staying in a place of comfort but uncomfortable inside. Do you fight for the family? Do you stay in the marriage? Does the church direct your path? Will the congregation shun you? Are you supposed to do the right thing? And what might that be?

My clients know that I will tell them to process these emotions of shame and guilt and leave them behind. Say it out loud, "Be done with it." Apologize only once or twice, but then from the heart. Others will "love" you and strangle you with their love, with their emotional blackmail, throwing you back in an abyss of expectations and rewards. To escape these bindings, you must move forwards. For yourself, on your own path. Without a doubt, my God wanted me to live my life in joy and peace, so I could be ready for the next task ahead. That is the "all about you" chapter of your life, where you have shed the old operating systems, the conditioning, and gotten busy with that which you need to do to come to a place of giving and sharing.

28

—·—

FALL IN RESPECT

Are you a person who likes to save others instead of looking inside at their own deep soul? For me, that was certainly the case, though I was not aware that that was what I was doing. My relationships started sometimes from a place of empathy. I would put myself in their shoes, moving from a shared experience and a deep understanding of what the other person was going through. I would even try to dig deeper and offer sometimes wanted and sometimes unwanted solutions. It is a wonderful place for me. I felt so needed, wanted, and important when I showed up as the lifesaver. A wonderful place for one's self-esteem and confidence. A wonderful step to fulfill a need to be seen and admired is to become indispensable to someone else. However, this was not a good place from which to care for myself.

Now, I teach my clients to see that a place of sympathy or sorrow is a healthier place, a place of understanding from your own perspective. This is a very different way of showing up for another, and if one is not careful, it could create more distance or look superficial if perceived as just pity. But that has to do with your skills and experience to communicate from a place of compassion. Nonetheless, whether it's a marriage or friendship, not taking on each other's emotional journeys as your own is a healthier base for survival.

I can see I could never communicate from a healthy place of friendship and partnership if it started with me viewing myself as the superhero or the victim. My deepest understanding of my warped relationships came way after they had ended. (Go figure, right?!) It was at this point that I clearly saw that the start was wrong, and my needy self was acting from a place of doubt and loneliness. The beginning might not be a good or healthy place, but we don't recognize that in the overwhelming sensations of loving, fun, and cuddles. We don't start a relationship telling the other party that they are good for 5 to 10 years. We always say, *"You are forever,"* and we mean it deeply at that moment. Years later, once the false dynamics had settled in, I could see how I would take someone's power away and disable them by wanting to be in control of everything. Yes, my motives were a desire to help someone change for the better, but I did not know that change won't happen if *they* don't want to change, too. And besides that, I found it funny that change can be a dirty word, but if we replace that with "growth" or "growing together," it is perceived as acceptable and as a challenge to work on the relationship.

Then there is love, which in my "coach myself" book was replaced by respect. I have found love in so many places and in so many ways, with family, with friendships, with partners and husbands in a short or long amount of time. But as soon as I lost respect for their character, I lost all love for them (regardless as to how good looking or rich they were). And then it is really over. It builds resentment, irritation, and anger, which leads to anxiety, depression, and unhappiness. The anxiety is always geared to not knowing what waits tomorrow, or how to handle the future. You can't imagine five years from now as a happy place. Depression comes in when emotions of indifference settle in, a dangerous place of not caring and thinking that no one cares about you anymore.

The unconditional and mutual love I finally found was based on respect and interest, a deep curiosity in the whereabouts of the other person, in the *why* behind our relationship, and the motivation behind the other person. It is balanced and a mutual decision to give and receive, to allow the other to care and to understand that they truly do. Not so much about how much I love, but more about how much I am being loved and allowing and accepting that beautiful feeling. From this place, we grow together, moving towards an exciting future, filling in the next five years with emotions of joy and exciting curiosity. I don't worry anymore. Instead, I feel concerned at times, and that is normal and human in times of distress or pain. Adding trust, shared faith and a joyful outlook on the future is a place for a mutually balanced relationship based on respect for each other.

29

BE BORING AND HEALTHY

T aking care of myself is something that I had to learn as I moved from exterior care to interior care. Self-care is not "selfies." It has nothing to do with self-indulgence nor with the Instagram culture of self-exposure.

Self-care also goes beyond your health, doctors' appointments, healthy habits in nutrition and diet, the occasional manicure or pedicure, and beauty regimens. In the past it was related to looking good with six pack abs, skinny bodies, expensive or creative wardrobes, and an exterior approach to look good in others' eyes. Taking care of myself became a more interior journey, related to a mind-body-spirit perspective, where my overall health encompassed balancing constant affirmations and self-empowerment as well as a loving look at my own body. I could be beautiful, despite my scoliosis back that I was hiding in oversized clothes. I could accept my long legs and short upper body and accept that one can be perfectly imperfect. I read this powerful quote from poet Nayyirah Waheed and felt it was written for me:

And I said to my body, softly, 'I want to be your friend.' It took a long breath and replied, 'I have waited my whole life for this'.

My physical shortcomings could become assets in my work, and I could become an example of a fitness expert with a handicap. It didn't hold me back from trying to do what others believed to be impossible, so why not use it as a story to empower others?

Self-love, self-acceptance and self-care is maintaining the inner self, listening and caring, being compassionate and open to opinions and differences. I learned to breathe, take a moment, be still, meditate and listen, pray and ask. I learned to discover where my body holds the pain, the trauma, stress, anxiety or fear. Learning to find, feel, accept and heal is an important aspect of understanding somatic symptoms, relating to our body as distinct from the mind. In any part of my work, understanding the relationship between the mind, body and spirit is crucial to helping and healing my patients and clients.

Living an honest and authentic life means paying bills on time, maintaining friendships, maintaining your health and your material belongings. I am frequently falling off the wagon but aware of it, and always aiming to get back on. I have the choice to act instead of to react, to respond with caution, turn obstacles into opportunities, creating every step on the way myself, sometimes in agreement with significant others.

When we are creating awareness, it becomes easier to catch ourselves in the moment, and change any habit that is no longer serving us toward that which we desire. This is based not only on my studies but also on that which I have internalized on my own journey. To clarify, information alone doesn't mean anything till you feel what it means and start doing something with it, correct? In other words, we need constant repetition. My patients might tell me that they have heard it all before, that the information shared becomes redundant. I answer them that I can't recite the bible and have been in church for decades. And the bible is only one book.

We need time and repetition to understand, comprehend, and make it our own. From there on we can share with others what that bit of wisdom has done for us and how it changed us, and made us a better person.

What must precede that step is, as I have taught for years, becoming more mindful (something that is no longer a given in our society). We are so overwhelmed with information overload and thus less able to retain information. Mindfulness practices have assumed different forms over the millennia though their purpose remains the same: to end suffering, stress, anxiety, and depression, and to enhance wellbeing. The current wave of mindfulness therapies, coaching, exercises, etc., owe most to a mindfulness-based, stress-reduction program developed in the late 1970s by, a professor of medicine emeritus at the University of Massachusetts.

I remember how my mother would come home and describe people she saw by the shape of their nose, eyes, or eyebrows, the color of their clothes or the shape of their shoes. Imagine if we had to describe someone now. Science has proven that we are bound by just a few features and miss out on the rest. Even though I had a hard time "seeing and remembering," nowadays I love to practice techniques to help myself and my clients improve their level of insight and mindfulness.

30

— · —

BE A REBEL WITH A CAUSE

The last point I'd like to make, to save you tons of time, energy, and misery, is that I lived my life according to what others expected or their imaginary opinions of me. With a permanent fake smile and an extreme work ethic, I strove daily for approval and acceptance and was not always true to myself and my own wants and needs. Everyone is guilty of this at some point in life, and this is perfectly normal provided that we recognize and celebrate our own intellect and development. Common sense? Not an easy thing to do, and it requires the will power and time to take a deep look at the self. Emotional intelligence is an ability to sense, understand, and effectively apply the power and acumen of emotions as judgment and decision making to connection and influence. I was not aware of my skills to perceive, understand, integrate, and manage my own and other people's feelings and emotions, nor to act upon them in a reflective manner. Everyone needs a sense of belonging, but we cannot force it, as I experienced many times. I was still the outsider and foreigner in a small-town church or library. I was still different in my approach to teaching or entertaining. Looking back, all my efforts made perfect sense. I wanted to please others to be accepted. Understanding that others perceived me in a different way was not always easy, but it was *exactly* what I created. If I didn't like to show my vulnerability, I would not share my story. And in my refusal to share, I built a wall around me.

I most definitely was perceived by some as arrogant, distant, or strong, although these things were totally opposite from what I really felt. Sometimes it led to a change in relationships with the ones I cared for. Few understood me, and it took me a while to fully know myself as well. It was not until I was in my forties that I realized that I am (in the depths of my being) a rebel *with* a cause. I will never forget the moment when a yoga student told me I should have asked for more money than I did. My information had been so precious to her, and my current prices undermined my value. Right there, I realized that I was not doing myself a favor. I had a hard time understanding that it is ok to acknowledge your accomplishments and add value to what you have done. For me, it is not easy, especially with deep, traditional, embedded beliefs about modesty, caretaking and complacency. It was about darn time to be my own best friend and to fully embrace myself, my body, and my success. Looking back now, my frustrations, my insecurities and the search for happiness all make perfect sense.

The confusing part of being a rebel with a cause though is that there are two main dynamics at play. A rebel with a cause likes to be different, break the rules, and act up while also changing the world for the better. I live from both of these places and with a heightened level of self-awareness, knowledge, and mindfulness, have learned to love and embrace both parts of me. It's about finding a way to channel your inner child, your energy in a productive way, so that your purpose becomes clear and a way of serving others.

All those years I wasted making every decision based on impressing or appeasing others. How arrogant of me to think that I could read minds? That I might have known what they were thinking? I had no idea what they were thinking, nor was it controllable if I ever figured it out. All that is controllable is my own thoughts and reactions. I don't want to regret lacking the courage to live a true life for myself. I want to have the courage to authentically express my feelings. I like to attract the people, places, and happenings in my life and not seek or wait for them.

I am, unapologetically, a rebel with a cause.

Forget following the rules of the game perfectly. From a love of self, God, and others, I'm playing a totally different game now, finding my way back from the expectations of others.

If you've read this far and realized that our paths ran parallel and are a woman who is forty or older, who wants to get your sexy back through emotional and physical health and wellness by moving trauma and pain that has been stored within for too long, even if you don't know what you want, will figure it out, while connecting with God in a new, holistic way, and without buying a plane ticket to India, I AM NEVER FAR AWAY, and it would be my joy to serve you.

elianhaan.com or connect with me on social media.

May your life be joyful and blessed, and may you be grateful for both.

WRAP PARTY

THANK YOU NOTES TO FAMILY, FRIENDS AND INFLUENCERS

I wish I would have spent more time with you

I wish I would have made more time for you

You mean more to me than I expressed

★★★

In loving kindness, I would like to extend my deepest love and gratitude to all listed below

A huge thanks to my family because I chose to move far away and distance became permanent. To my aunts and uncles who helped in dark times. To my sister, Loes, who I love so much and my niece, Youssra, who is courageous, smart, and strong. I wish I had known you both better then and was there for you when you needed me. We will have to make up time.

Thanks to my cousins for a great childhood and endless summers. Thanks to my high school and Dance Academy friends, Roosmarie Ruigrok and Roel Voorintholt, for sharing my love for dancing throughout life. To Theater School and University friends who believed in me, worked with and for me, and saw my gifts way before I did.

Thanks to Mieke Peters for becoming the most loyal, lifetime friend and wise advisor anyone can wish for. To my first love, for growing up with me (although too fast) and showing me a big part of the world. To best friends and "brothers," Leopold and Ruud, for always being there when I needed you most. To my Keu friends and customers for years of fun and hard work.

Thanks to Mariette and Claudia for being there for me in hard times of loss and fun times of exploring the city of Amsterdam in the summers. To Willemien and Petra who worked beside me, joined me in long nights of pool tournaments, music events, and even came to the States to check on me and always stayed in touch. And to Heleen, Fred, Iris, and Jan Willem who checked in for support and comfort after pain.

Thanks to Karen & Jo Sebbag for giving me a new United States family, to TJ Mete for adopting me, to Trushar, Frida, and Gabrielle for your love and encouragement to move on in a new country. To Elfriede Russell, for showing me grace and beauty, a shared love for the arts and theater, for your support and fun in Los Angeles. To Bob Cowley (cheers to you in heaven), Tara Di Leva, Shannon Zimlich, Marion Trent, and Brian Peterman for laughter, your always open door homes, and for showing me show business like no one else can. Thank you Bill Rhoten, for still asking me to join your theatre productions. To my (and my son's) talent agent, Linda MacAlister, for believing in my talent, skills, and determination, and for embracing my journey.

Thanks to the Kemp Methodist Church family, for making me feel at home in a new and unknown world of country and cowboys. To Pearl for showing up as my "sister" in enthusiasm and a shared optimistic determination to save the world on a daily basis. And to Carolyn Long for believing in my creativity, my talent, and my ongoing wishes to grow and change the world.

Thanks to Rhett and the Bakke and Lorenzetti family, for showing our son unconditional love and support. To Ole for being the best sub-grandpa my son could wish for.

Thanks to all you very special and loyal students of Better Body Basics. You have no idea how much I learned from you all these years. You have been supportive followers of my endeavors. Kari and Cindy, you make me feel proud in friendship and in yoga. Lynda, Linda, Vicky, and Bob our friendship has sustained beyond studio hours, and there are so many more to thank.

To my Athens Tai Chi friends, how I love you and miss you. Kay Moore for continuing a beautiful group in movement. Paula Lemmon and Carolyn Brinkman, creative and strong women, why did I not make more time for your wise words. Thanks to Vinnie Stromolo's leadership and my Treehouse friends who all had such a huge impact on my personal and professional growth and helped set the stage for my ultimate purpose to help others and change lives.

Thanks to SCW fitness CEO Sara Kooperman, for allowing me the opportunity to join your world tours and the best in the business. Thanks to Connie Martin for inviting me to the MOVE conventions. Lawrence Biscontini, Irene Mc-Cormick, Keli Roberts, Ann Gilbert, Mindy Mylrea, Melissa Lane and Leslee Bender, you were all such an inspiration to me in the fitness world. I breathe your words as I continue to be a believer and perfect clone of your creations and knowledge. Thanks to Tricia Silverman, Lisa Gibson, Bernadette O'Brien, Jane Traceski, Christine Conti, and Billie Wartenberg for making me feel at home and respected in my profession. You made me feel special and welcome in a world of hotel rooms and trade shows.

Thank you Nan and Ed, for many wonderful celebrations at your beautiful home and for putting us at the table together, encouraging me to date the fabulous Mr. Fabulous. You were supportive and encouraging when no one else believed. The original queens, for keeping me in the best company when changes were so rough.

Thanks to my ever so loving, accepting and supporting Church family, who witnessed my son grow up from a skipping, young kid to a strong, intelligent, and kind human being. You taught me the extent of sharing God's message, discipleship, strength in faith, the power of prayer, and kindness without boundaries.

Thanks to Meg Calvin, my writing coach, for your talent, ongoing support, and love for my story. I wouldn't have believed a word I said without your witty remarks, guidance, and encouragement.

Thank you Jim and Keagan, my loves, for putting up with me at all times. For loving me more than I can handle, encouraging me to write my story, following up with relentless support during everyday chores and sleepless nights. You have taught me everything I needed to know about being loved and accepting in grace.

Thank you to all I missed here; you are in my heart

And finally, a huge thank you hug in heaven to Lee Peterson, who was my acting coach, tough, rough, and beautiful inside and out. You gave me the courage to share my story and made me believe in the greater good of doing so. I miss your honesty, your punches, the ones that I needed to make me believe and shine.

Thank you, dearest Lee P, for handing me the title of this book.

ENDORSEMENTS

As a presenter for SCW Mania Conventions for fitness professionals, Elian demonstrated the ability to capture and inspire large audiences from coast to coast. With her now well known "coach approach" to move, move forwards and move up, Elian makes complex fitness concepts and life lessons easy to understand for attendees of all genres and ages. Her exotic accent and injection of appropriate humor captivates her audiences, and she continues to inspire through global movement seminars, a weekly tv show and in her work as coach and counselor.

Sara Kooperman, CEO, SCW Fitness Education, waterinm otion.com, seatfitness.com

When I met Elian at our treatment Ranch in Texas I knew after a couple of minutes that she had the energy and spirit to complete my Mind, Body, Spirit treatment program and philosophy. Her Wellness program was an integral part of our success.

Vinnie Strumolo, CEO, LMFT, Resolutions Healthcare

I am proud to know Elian and to have worked with her. She graced our Stage in Barefoot in the Park and Damn Yankees and choreographed several dance numbers. She is always there to help others. Thanks Lady.

Bill Rhoten, Theatre Rocks, artistic Director, Producer, Actor, Playwright

"I did not think that I could ever get rid of my negative self-talk but working with Elian has helped me to love and accept ALL parts of me (even the parts I used to run from). If you are ready for more confidence and a deeper connection to God, then read her book, attend her workshops, watch her show or hire her today!"

Meg Calvin, Bestselling Author, and Coach

About Author

Elian Haan stole the show on stage and screen as a global dancer, presenter and actress who performed on such sets as *Walker, Texas Ranger* before eventually producing her own TV show. In this memoir with a twist, Elian's life off-camera was just as, if not more, riveting than anything on screen.

As a child with severe skeletal issues in a family with enough skeletons in the closet, Netherland-born Elian was searching for God in all directions, but he didn't seem to care about what she wanted. This, on top of all else, made her really good at faking a smile. Her acting skills served her well as she hid an eating disorder while consumed with her parent's drama. Coming of age in the heavy blurred lines of professional dance and fitness, she tried many hats in order to be taken seriously as a Barbie blonde.

Despite such ridiculous moments as her husband leaving her for her best friend after following him "across the pond," stranger-than-fiction lawsuits, and many late-night encounters and spiritual adventures, she finally found herself and her Jesus in the mess and transformed into a sought-after motivational speaker, yoga instructor, and life coach who has helped thousands move through trauma and addiction.

Now known as "the official energy healer and dealer," she's here with her "Elianisms" with the hopes of guiding you to:

- Reclaim and honor the mental, physical, and spiritual connection as a Christian

- Remember that your body is your best friend

- Officially drop out of the game of keeping up appearances

- Stop taking things personally

- Remove trauma and pain that has been stored in the body

- Create healthy boundaries within toxic relationships

- Increase self-trust and self-love, *all while laughing as you learn.*

This comforting and cathartic read explores such questions as:

1. What role does humor have in moving the pain of past hurts?

2. Should the doctor be the alternative healthcare, while our first steps in well-care are found in simply breathing, movement, and herbal remedies?

3. What are some practical steps to take to stop being a people-pleaser and become a Jesus-pleaser?

4. Is the secret to a happy life *really* to take a different lover every ten years?

5. Do you have to be a late bloomer in order to be an awesome parent?

6. Do you have to live on the prairie without WiFi and hairspray to rediscover your inner strength, or can you learn to go against the grain of our modern, instant-gratification culture right where you are?

Elian Haan is an author, TV show host of "Elian's Joy," and international motivational speaker and presenter. Born in the Netherlands, she moved in her thirties to the USA, trained in dance, theater, arts, and fitness. She has spent most of her professional life in the fitness and wellness industry and is a Certified Life Coach with a yoga studio and private practice in Texas. Elian has always focused on helping people feel healthy and well, and you can find her mind-body-spirit "Coach Approach" on the international stage presenting her own fitness and wellness programs. Besides her studio classes and private practice, she has worked as wellness counselor with trauma and addiction patients at a Texas inpatient rehab facility since 2015.

Elian is specialized in pain management and anxiety intervention, and certified in many specialty programs for addiction recovery, trauma informed yoga and energy work, somatic therapy (a mind-body approach to stress and trauma) and remedial and corrective exercise. She resides with her Mr. Fabulous in Texas and follows her amazing son in all his adventures.

You can find her on her website www.elianhaan.com

www.ingramcontent.com/pod-product-compliance
Lightning Source LLC
Chambersburg PA
CBHW070658130626
46553CB00005B/1758

* 9 7 9 8 2 1 8 0 4 9 7 6 8 *